LOWERING THE WALL:
RELIGION AND THE SUPREME COURT IN THE 1980s

BY
GREGG IVERS

Anti-Defamation League
823 United Nations Plaza
New York, NY 10017

Library of Congress Catalog Number 91-61870

ISBN—0-88464-139-2

**This publication has been made possible through a grant
of the Harry H. Lipsig Endowment Fund.**

ACKNOWLEDGEMENTS

The idea for this book began over lunch two years ago while I was in New York City on other business. Jill Kahn, the Associate Director of the Legal Affairs Department of the Anti-Defamation League of B'nai B'rith, mentioned to me that ADL was interested in having an independent scholar write a book on the changes which had developed in church-state law during the 1980s. My response was that I did not think church-state law under this Supreme Court had developed much at all, but had instead taken a giant—and unwelcome step—backward. I suggested that perhaps ADL should find someone whose views were more in accord with its own. Then Jill paid for lunch and said, "We have, if you want to do it." Having just been relieved of the cost of lunch in New York City, I had no choice but to accept.

Jill did more than just offer me the chance to write this book. She guided me through from start to finish, making available the resources of her precise legal mind and skilled editorial hand at all times. Her continual prodding, encouragement and support sustained the book to its completion. To her, I offer my genuine heartfelt appreciation for all that she did to redeem whatever merits this book might have. I also want to thank Steven Freeman, Richard Shevitz and Ruti Teitel for their constructive criticism on earlier drafts of this book. The professionalism of the entire legal staff of ADL deserves praise for their willingness to respond to my numerous requests on how to improve the book while remaining unintrusive in steering its editorial content.

Several other colleagues and friends read the manuscript, numerous others listened to me discuss it, and many more answered my questions about the current direction of church-state law, all of whom provided helpful suggestions that helped to clear up my thinking on the subject. Especially helpful were Jack Rossotti of American University; Karen O'Connor of Emory University; Brent Walker, Associate Counsel for the Baptist Joint Committee; Eric Mazur, formerly a Public Policy Fellow at the American Jewish Committee; Rabbi David Saperstein of the Union of American Hebrew Congregations; Dean Kelley of the National Council of Churches; and Marc Stern of the American Jewish Congress.

Without the excellent and energetic assistance of several research assistants and former students, I would have still been wandering around the libraries tracking down information, verifying facts, checking citations and doing all the other unglamorous tasks that enabled me to complete this book much sooner than had I been resolved to fend for myself. Thank you Karen Ehatt, Tim Evanson, Amy Sobel, Marc Zwillinger and Judy Levenson for all your help.

In between the conception and completion of this book, Janet Krell once again endured one unsolicited monologue after another on obscure legal cases, judicial politics and the health and welfare of the Supreme Court. Nonetheless, she still agreed to and then did marry me. Her patience, love and understanding always make what I do much easier.

Finally, I dedicate this book to the best father a son could ever have, Mike Ivers. For it is he who first taught me the value of an idea and the idea of values.

Gregg Ivers
April 15, 1991

TABLE OF CONTENTS

FOREWORD

Gregg Ivers, Assistant Professor of Government at American University, has written a highly informative and cautionary book that is required reading for all those concerned about religious liberty in America—lawyers and non-lawyers alike. It is on the one hand an exhilarating read, as the author guides us through the historic development of the U.S. Supreme Court's commitment to the twin concepts embodied in the First Amendment's religion clauses: separation of church and state and freedom of religion. It is, on the other hand, a sobering read, as the author demonstrates that during the 1980s, in case after case, the Court significantly departed from those basic constitutional values.

The Supreme Court, of course, was not operating in a vacuum. The last decade, beginning with Ronald Reagan's inauguration into the presidency, saw the rise and political empowerment of religious fundamentalism in American society. Fundamentalist groups, with the open backing of the Reagan Administration, sought to reintroduce prayer in the public schools, to influence the content of school curricula and textbooks, and to benefit from government largesse in a myriad of ways, from aid to parochial schools to religious displays at public expense. At the same time, intolerance for non-majoritarian religious beliefs and practices grew.

While the fundamentalist movement has not been successful in securing approval for every item on its agenda, the Rehnquist Court has been far more hospitable to its claims than were the Warren and Burger Courts. As Professor Ivers describes the major Establishment Clause decisions of the 1980s, one is struck by the inexorable erosion of 40 years of precedent as the new, "conservative" majority on the Court strains to accommodate majoritarian religious politics. In the process, the Court not only disregards longstanding Supreme Court precedents but also, even more disturbingly, it undermines the Constitution's barriers against governmental involvement with religion.

The Constitutional Framers sought to preserve religion as a sphere for private choice and autonomy, as to which government was to maintain neutrality. Through the two religion clauses, the Founders enjoined both governmental support for religion and governmental encroachments upon religion. It is, therefore, ironic that

Justices who in other contexts profess fidelity to judicial restraint, the plain language of the Constitution, and the original intent of the Framers nevertheless depart from those conservative tenets in the crucial area of religion.

The most dramatic and disturbing example of the Rehnquist Court's judicial activism in rewriting constitutional history regarding religion was its 1990 decision in *Oregon v. Smith*. As Professor Ivers forcefully demonstrates, in this decision the Rehnquist majority stretched to overturn long-settled precepts of free exercise jurisprudence that the parties had not even raised, let alone addressed. Thus, without any advance notice to the litigants or the larger affected public, and without any briefs or oral arguments on point, the Court substantially reinterpreted the Free Exercise Clause in such a way as to endanger the religious liberty of all who adhere to non-majoritarian faiths.

The *Smith* majority opinion candidly acknowledges that its reasoning would eliminate the Free Exercise Clause's role as the guarantor of religious liberty for adherents of minority religions, relegating their freedom to the good will of legislative majorities. The majority's explanation that discriminatory truncation of the constitutional rights of minority groups is the "unavoidable consequence of democratic government" shirks the Court's historic responsibility to avoid those very consequences.

It is worth recalling the frequently quoted words of Justice Jackson in *West Virginia Board of Education v. Barnette*, which was a landmark case in establishing not only religious liberty, but also the Supreme Court's special role in protecting Bill of Rights freedoms more generally:

> The very purpose of the Bill of Rights was to withdraw certain subjects from the vicissitudes of political controversy, to place them beyond the reach of majorities and officials and to establish them as legal principles to be applied by the courts. One's right to life, liberty, and property, to free speech, a free press, freedom of worship and assembly, and other fundamental rights may not be submitted to a vote; they depend on the outcome of no elections.

Smith's unanticipated assault on the First Amendment prompted an unprecedently broad coalition of constitutional scholars, as well as religious, civil liberties, and other groups to petition the Court for a rehearing. This request was, however, denied.

In short, the deference that the Rehnquist Court has shown toward majoritarian religious beliefs has not extended to unorthodox or minority religions. Jews, Black Muslims and Native Americans have all received short shrift from the current Court, which has tended to minimize the importance of their deeply held religious beliefs while exaggerating the importance of countervailing governmental interests. In the author's words, religious freedom "enters the 1990s relegated to the unaccustomed and unforeseen position of second-class stature in our constellation of constitutional values."

The American Civil Liberties Union, along with the Anti-Defamation League and a handful of other civil liberties groups, will continue to shoulder much of the burden of defending the First Amendment's religion clauses against further depredations. Professor Gregg Ivers' important book will not only inform the public debate over these critical issues, but will also light the way for those of us whose work is not yet finished.

Nadine Strossen
President
American Civil Liberties Union

April 1991

INTRODUCTION

Congress shall make no law respecting an establishment of religion, or prohibiting the free exercise thereof. . . .

The First Amendment

In 1947, when the Anti-Defamation League of B'nai B'rith filed its first *amicus*— "friend of the court"—brief in the Supreme Court of the United States, it was to argue that releasing children from classes to provide them with religious education on the premises of public schools violated the First Amendment's establishment clause. ADL's early victory in *McCollum v. Board of Education* was followed by decades of advocacy before the Supreme Court on issues of church-state separation and religious freedom.

ADL's staunch support of the establishment and free exercise clauses has often been criticized—as have similar activities of other religious and civil rights organizations. Groups arguing for strict separation between government and religion have been variously accused of being "anti-religion" and promoting the religion of "secular humanism." Those seeking religious accommodation and protection have been charged with encouraging favoritism. Nevertheless, our position in the areas of establishment and free exercise has been unwavering because it evolves from the agency's founding mandate to "secure justice and fair treatment to all citizens alike."

The Anti-Defamation League was established in 1913 and has worked continuously as a defender and protector of the Jewish community. Integral to that effort is an understanding that the rights of any individual are dependent upon the protection accorded all minorities. Unless every American is free to worship—or not—at his or her own discretion, religious freedom is jeopardized for every one of us. The Founding Fathers, recognizing that this country was established by individuals seeking religious freedom, incorporated this guarantee in the First Amendment to the U.S. Constitution.

The Jewish community is all too aware of the dangers of a partnership between government and religion; the Spanish Inquisition is only one example of Jewish suffering at the hands of state-sponsored religion. In the words of Justice Hugo Black, the "first and most immediate purpose [of the establishment clause] rested on the belief that a union of government and religion tends to destroy government and to degrade religion."

XI

In 1984, ADL issued a report on legislative and judicial developments in church-state relations which noted that the traditional "wall of separation" was, if not crumbling, becoming "transparent." The accuracy of that observation has, unfortunately, been confirmed. While there have been isolated victories in the areas of establishment and free exercise conflicts, the Supreme Court is clearly shifting from a strict interpretation of the First Amendment's religion clauses.

Professor Gregg Ivers presents the reader not only with an informative and insightful analysis of church-state litigation over the past decade, but also with a challenge. His conclusion that decisions in the 1980s significantly weakened the vitality of the First Amendment's religion clauses challenges all those committed to religious freedom to remain vigilant and to support efforts to stem further erosion of constitutional protection.

Melvin Salberg   Abraham H. Foxman
National Chairman   National Director

CHAPTER ONE

RELIGION AND POLITICS
IN THE 1980s

Alexis de Tocqueville, the astute French aristocrat whose analysis of American social and political institutions in the early 19th century remains astonishingly fresh to this day, noted that Americans varied widely in their attachment to religion, but universally believed that the health and vibrancy of religious institutions were essential, even indispensable, to the maintenance and progress of a democratic society. Tocqueville believed that the mores and values associated with religion were so deeply embedded in American public and private life that he concluded religion should be considered the first of all American institutions. Religious doctrines differed in their form and manner of worship, but were in agreement concerning the basic values that should underlie the moral foundation of civil government—personal and economic liberty, individual dignity and the moral obligation of individuals to enhance their community and country. Religion did not intervene directly in the governing of American society; instead it provided the basis for the civic virtue and enlightened self-interest necessary to a liberal, democratic society dependent upon reason and choice, not violence and force, for its survival and prosperity.

The respect for religious differences and the strength of organized religion in America, Tocqueville also believed, stemmed from the twin constitutional principles of religious disestablishment and liberty of conscience found in the religion clauses of the First Amendment to the United States Constitution, which requires that "Congress shall make no law respecting an establishment of religion, or prohibiting the free exercise thereof." Free from the coercive and potentially corrupt influence of the state, organized religion prospered in America and still maintained, in his view, a "quiet sway over the country because of the complete separation of church and state." [1] Furthermore, Tocqueville wrote that, "as long as religion derives its strength from sentiments, instincts and passion, it can brave the assaults of time. But when a religion chooses to rely on the interests of the world, it becomes almost as fragile as all earthly powers. . .hence any alliance with any political power whatsoever is bound to be burdensome for religion. It does not need their support in order to live, and in serving them it may die." [2]

In the American constitutional arrangement of separated and divided power, the federal courts, particularly the Supreme Court, historically have been responsible for quelling the majoritarian impulses emanating from Congress and the state legislatures, whether designed to provide government aid to sectarian institutions or support for religious preferences in the public realm. For almost four decades, the Court stood fast against legislative action whose benefits were intended for religious majorities, and led a legal revolution that elevated the status of religious minorities from an existence on the constitutional margins to one of full and equal membership in the American cultural and religious milieu. But if trends emergent in the Supreme Court at the close of the 1980s are indicative of new thinking about the relationship between government and religion, there is reason to believe that, for religious minorities, the future is indeed portentous.

The Supreme Court and Religion

From the early 1940s, when it first articulated a set of guiding principles in both the free exercise and establishment clause areas, and continuing through the early 1980s, the Supreme Court slowly and steadily crafted a high wall of separation between organized religion and the state while also narrowing the reach of government power to regulate or impose sanctions for personal behavior associated with religious conduct. During those four decades, the Court struck down state-sponsored prayer and Bible recitation in the public schools,[3] direct financial aid to elementary and secondary parochial schools,[4] state statutes criminalizing the teaching of evolution or requiring the teaching of creationism,[5] and a state requirement mandating that public officials take religious oaths to assume public office.[6]

Furthermore, the Court, in another series of innovative and creative decisions, broadened the scope of religious free exercise to grant constitutional protection to unorthodox religious conduct that for years had fallen victim to legislative proscription. For example, the Court upheld conscientious objection to military service based on nonsectarian and nonreligious grounds,[7] ruled that unemployment compensation could not be denied to persons fired from their jobs or unable to obtain work because of a conflict with Sabbath observance or other religious beliefs[8] and exempted religious groups from state statutes regulating certain forms of civil and criminal conduct otherwise applicable to the greater population.[9] The cumulative impact of the religion clause decisions of the Warren and early Burger Courts on both church-state separation and religious freedom was, with a few exceptions, to transform from sand into brick the metaphorical wall that Thomas Jefferson, over 150 years before, argued should separate religious life from civil government.

However, the church-state jurisprudence of the Supreme Court in the 1980s has been the work of an uncertain stonemason. The decade witnessed an erratic but gradual erosion of the separationist principles which had once served as the intellectual rationale for the pathbreaking—and, for religious minorities, liberating— decisions of the Court a generation earlier. During the 1980s, the Court upheld state-sponsored Christmas Nativity and Chanukah Menorah displays on public and private property,[10] approved tax relief for parents who send their children to parochial schools,[11] permitted the use of government funds to support ceremonial invocation and prayer in state legislatures,[12] ruled that student-initiated religious clubs can meet in secondary public schools[13] and in public university facilities during nonclassroom hours[14] and sustained a congressional funding scheme that allocated federal grants to sectarian institutions providing sex education and counseling.[15]

The Court provided some reassurance that Clarence Darrow could rest in peace when it struck down a Louisiana law allowing public secondary schools to offer students a course in "creation-science" if they taught evolution as part of its science curriculum,[16] and reassured nervous separationists that its historic decisions of the early 1960s declaring state-sponsored school prayer unconstitutional were still good law by invalidating an Alabama statute permitting "voluntary prayer."[17] However, the Court indicated, in both cases, that "religion-neutral" statutes allowing "moments-of-silence" and the teaching of creationism in public schools might be acceptable if intended to promote a secular, educational purpose.[18] Moreover, that the view of Chief Justice Warren E. Burger supporting the notion that the Constitution *"affirmatively mandates accommodation, not merely tolerance, of all religions,"*[19] could command a majority of the Court in the mid-1980s signaled to separationists that the pending demise of a strict interpretation of the establishment clause had made the metamorphosis from unwelcome thought to unpleasant fact.

Equally unsettling in the religion clause jurisprudence of the Court was the increasing level of intolerance that it showed for the free exercise rights of minority religious observers. The Court denied the right of an Orthodox Jewish Air Force psychologist, who also was an ordained rabbi, to wear his yarmulke while on duty,[20] permitted the federal government to take property for public use that for years had been used as a sacred burial and ritual ground by Native Americans,[21] upheld the assignment of social security numbers to Native Americans and the imposition of social security taxes on the Amish, both groups having objected based on religious doctrine,[22] and limited the proselytizing rights of Hari Krishnas in public forums.[23] In the most devastating decision for religious freedom issued in the modern era, the Supreme Court ruled that states were not required to show a compelling governmental interest or less restrictive regulative means when refusing to uphold the religious free exercise rights of individuals whose conduct stemmed from sincerely held and recognized beliefs, but ran afoul of civil or criminal law. In the process, the Court overturned a doctrine that for almost thirty years had comprised the core of its free exercise jurisprudence.[24]

Not only did the Court become more sympathetic to legislative support for majoritarian religious beliefs and practices at the expense of religious minorities and nonbelievers during the 1980s, it substantially altered the purpose-effect-entanglement test it had developed in *Lemon v. Kurtzman (1971).*[25] In *Lemon*, the Court held that, to survive constitutional muster, a statute must not have a religious purpose, must not advance or inhibit religion and must not result in excessive entanglement between religious and state institutions.[26] The Court engaged in often heated internal bickering over what constituted a religious purpose or excessive entanglement, but a majority continued to apply the *Lemon* test in good faith. However, recent pronouncements of the late Burger and Rehnquist Courts indicate that the *Lemon* test is all but set for the constitutional guillotine.[27]

In one case, the Court abandoned the three-part *Lemon* test altogether,[28] and dropped not-so-subtle hints in several others that wholesale revisions in its establishment clause jurisprudence are in the offing.[29] For now, the Justice whose writings have proven to be most influential in shaping the contours of the new debate over the meaning of the religion clauses is Sandra Day O'Connor. Justice O'Connor is a vociferous critic of *Lemon*, but she does not share the enthusiasm of her more conservative colleagues that the Court jettison all juridical standards it has developed over time to analyze establishment clause cases. In perhaps her most significant contribution to constitutional jurisprudence since her elevation to the Court in 1981, Justice O'Connor is prepared to trim *Lemon* in order to focus "on institutional entanglement and on endorsement or disapproval of religion," which she believes "clarifies the *Lemon* test as an analytical device." [30] In Justice O'Connor's view, the purpose prong of the *Lemon* test should be modified to consider whether a statute actually endorses religion, not whether it merely possesses a religious purpose. Likewise, the second prong of *Lemon*, which prohibits governmental advancement or inhibition of religion, should focus on whether the effect of the law is to endorse or disapprove of religion. A statute would pass constitutional review under the establishment clause even if it advanced religion, so long as it did not explicitly endorse or disapprove of religion. [31]

On the surface, the endorsement test advanced by Justice O'Connor respects the institutional separation of religion and the state because it encompasses an analytical framework sensitive to statutes implicating the establishment clause. Even some commentators sympathetic to the strict separation of church and state have found little of the endorsement test with which to quarrel, arguing that it provides greater flexibility than *Lemon*. [32] Still, for several reasons, the movement of the Court towards O'Connor's endorsement standard is troubling. Her treatment of the purpose and effect prongs of *Lemon* would permit states to write legislation that grants assistance to or support of religion, as long as religion is not the central or sole institutional recipient of public benefits, or so long as the government has not lent its imprimatur to religious goals. Most recently, Justice O'Connor used the endorsement standard to reach her opinion in *Westside v. Mergens (1990)*, [33] in which the Court upheld the right of student religious clubs to meet in secondary public schools, on the basis that the fundamental purpose of the Equal Access Act of 1984 [34] was to promote student speech, even though she acknowledged that the legislation was intended to provide support for and advance the interest of student religion. [35] The more accommodating treatment given to religion under Justice O'Connor's jurisprudence means that legislation providing public assistance to parochial schools or support for other forms of state-sponsored religion in the public schools, such as moments-of-silence or religious curriculum, stand a far better chance than before of surviving constitutional scrutiny.

While Justice O'Connor has been out front in reshaping the church-state jurisprudence of the Court, the foremost figure leading the assault on its establishment clause decisions has been the new Chief Justice, William H. Rehnquist. Although Chief Justice Burger, particularly in the latter part of his tenure, gradually converted to the accommodationist wing of the Court, he never openly questioned the fundamental principles laid down by the establishment clause decisions of his Court or those before him. Chief Justice Rehnquist, on the other hand, has argued consistently since his appointment to the High Court in 1971 for a nonpreferential interpretation of the establishment clause. Illustrated best in his *Wallace v. Jaffree (1985)* dissent, Chief Justice Rehnquist believes that the establishment clause only prohibits the government from creating a national religion, or preferring one religion over another, but allows government to accommodate religion or dispense aid to religious institutions on a "neutral basis." [36]

Confined to a role that often found him issuing solo dissents in religion cases during his early years on the Court, Chief Justice Rehnquist, with the addition of Justices Antonin Scalia and Anthony Kennedy, both of whom are firm nonpreferentialists, now finds his views commanding a much wider acceptance among his colleagues. All three, apparently along with Justice White, are ready and willing to abandon the three-part *Lemon* test in favor of an approach more inclusive of what they argue is the proper historical and traditional context of the establishment clause than to the strict separation between religion and the state. [37] If only moderately successful in persuading the Court to tear down the Jeffersonian wall of separation, Chief Justice Rehnquist has triumphed in his once lone call for the Court to reconsider and perhaps reject altogether the analytic framework of its establishment clause jurisprudence. Moreover, he is a powerful and articulate jurist who is well-liked and well-respected by his colleagues across the ideological spectrum of the Court. Combined with the impressive leadership skills he has shown as a new Chief Justice, a Supreme Court led by William Rehnquist is in a formidable position to chart a new, quite possibly radical, course designed to challenge the constitutional boundaries separating religion from the state.

Congressional Action

For years, the politics of religion and state could best be understood by the competing interests that made the federal courts the locus of this conflict. Interest groups have dominated the ebb and flow of church-state litigation from the first religion clause decisions of the modern era, *Cantwell v. Connecticut (1940)*[38] and *Everson v. Board of Education (1947)*,[39] and have remained the controlling institutional force challenging religious preference statutes. [40] But the 1980s were a period that will be remembered as one in which conservatives rose to an influential position in American politics, one that went far beyond their newly-found power in the electoral process. Religious conservatives, encouraged by the election of Ronald Reagan, awoke from an era of political complacency fully prepared to enter high-powered Washington politics, including an arena long almost exclusively used by moderate and liberal groups to advance their policy objectives—the courts. This development startled the network of mainline religious lobbies that for so long had represented ecumenical dialogue in public affairs. Having taken considerable credit for the election of President Reagan and the first Republican majority in the Senate since 1954, conservative evangelicals and fundamentalists aimed their political sights at moving favorable legislation through Congress. Moreover, the new religious right had staunch allies in the plethora of other conservative organizations that came to Washington to set up shop in 1980, all of whom were better organized, more politically sophisticated and better financed than ever before. [41]

Most of the religion cases decided by the Supreme Court since the 1940s had arisen from challenges to state, not federal, law. Congress, due in some part to the express prohibition placed on it by the First Amendment, but in greater part to its desire to avoid legislating in areas where social divisiveness is inherent, historically had never demonstrated more than deferential attention to church-state issues, and when it had that action resembled political posturing more than genuine substantive concern over constitutional values. Even in the modern era of church-state relations, which commenced after *Everson*, Congress had scarcely shown any interest in the subject at all, preferring that any politically divisive matters involving church-state relations find their resolution in the courts. Faced with a powerful coalescence of evangelical and fundamentalist forces representative of the broad wave of conservative religious populism which had swept the country, Congress found itself pressured to accommodate their demands for prayer in the public schools, financial assistance to parochial institutions for an array of social services and to secure legislation allowing student religious clubs equal access to public school facilities. Congress, in turn, in responded.

The Adolescent Family Life Act of 1981

In 1981, Congress passed the Adolescent Family Life Act, a successor to the Adolescent Health Services and Pregnancy Prevention Act of 1978. [43] The AFLA provided direct federal grants to public and nonprofit agencies, including organizations with ties to religious bodies, for services and research in the area of premarital adolescent sexual relations and pregnancy. The AFLA also prohibited funding to any institution that performed abortions, abortion counseling, or that advocated, promoted or encouraged abortion.

Although many secular and religious groups opposed the AFLA, including organizations such as the American Civil Liberties Union and People for the American Way and an interfaith coalition of Christians and Jews, it passed through Congress with little opposition. Opponents of the AFLA argued that only those religious and religiously-affiliated organizations that advocated abstinence in premarital relations and opposed abortion under all circumstances were eligible for federal funding. [44] These conditions for statutory eligibility, in the view of the AFLA opponents, limited the distribution of federal funds to religious organizations whose positions on procreational and abortion policy were intertwined with religious doctrine. Congress undoubtedly has a legislative interest in providing federal assistance to public and private agencies for the sexual education of adolescents, but it has no constitutional authorization under the First Amendment to supplement the advancement of inherently sectarian instruction on matters related to sexual conduct.

Moreover, the AFLA amended the Public Adolescent Health Services and Pregnancy Prevention and Care Act of 1978 expressly to permit funding to religious organizations. The pressure to include religious institutions among the federal recipients was a result of a concerted lobbying effort by anti-abortion religious lobbies, such as the United States Catholic Conference, Concerned Women for America and the Moral Majority. In light of the campaign support that many legislators had received from conservative religious lobbies in the 1980 election, it is not surprising that Congress so willingly submitted to their desire to enlist federal support in an area of social policy that previously had been restricted to secular social welfare agencies. Perhaps more telling, the fact that pro-choice Protestant, Jewish and Catholic organizations received little or no AFLA funding due to their policies on sex education and abortion counseling further highlights the suspect motives of the legislation. [45] That it narrowly survived an establishment clause challenge in the Supreme Court gives added pause to future efforts of the federal government to intervene in related areas of social services.

The School Prayer Amendment Debates of 1983-84

The second major church-state showdown of the 1980s was an attempt by Congress to overturn almost 25 years of Supreme Court decisions that struck down state-supported prayer and other devotional exercises in the public schools. Encouraged by a letter President Reagan had sent to his supporters in the religious community during his reelection campaign of 1983-84 pledging his support for a constitutional amendment to school prayer, the evangelical and fundamentalist lobbies began to pressure Congress soon afterwards to take action on a school prayer amendment. [46] By the summer of 1983, the Senate opened hearings on two separately proposed school prayer amendments to the Constitution. The first proposal, submitted by the Reagan Administration, read, "Nothing in this Constitution shall be construed to prohibit individual or group prayer in public schools or other public institutions. Neither the United States nor any State shall compose the words of any prayer to be said in the public schools." The second proposal, sponsored by Senator Orrin Hatch (R-UT), contained similar language, but modified the Administration proposal somewhat by substituting the phrase, "group silent prayer or meditation" for "individual or group prayer."

In March 1984, the Senate Judiciary Committee brought the Reagan Administration's version to the floor for a vote. After considerable and often acrimonious debate, much of which consisted of speeches written for the Senators by the different religious interests at play, the entire Senate voted 56-44 in favor of the school prayer amendment, falling 11 votes shy of the two-thirds majority necessary for the passage of a constitutional amendment. The tally reflected only marginal crossover voting, with the new Republican majority largely supporting the Administration proposal and the Democratic minority opposing it. Nonetheless, that 56 Senators were willing to vote to overturn the school prayer cases[47] through a constitutional amendment was an indication that federal legislation providing a less conspicuous means of securing accommodation of student worship in the public schools would most likely have little trouble obtaining congressional support.

The Equal Access Act of 1984

Having failed in a direct attempt to restore organized prayer in the public schools through a constitutional amendment, Republicans in Congress and President Reagan subsequently turned their newly-found enthusiasm for religion in the public schools to legislative remedies. Using as a legal baseline the decision of the Supreme Court in *Widmar v. Vincent (1981)*,[48] which struck down a long-standing policy of the University of Missouri Board of Regents that prohibited student religious clubs from using its facilities for meeting purposes, Congress attempted in late 1982 to secure protection for the right of student religious clubs to hold meetings on public school grounds through the introduction of the Religious Speech Protection Act. The Religious Speech Protection Act required all public secondary schools receiving federal funding to permit student religious clubs to meet on campus if they also allowed non-school sponsored groups access to school facilities. Cosponsored by Senator Mark Hatfield (R-OR) and Representative Don Bonker (D-WA), the Religious Speech Protection Act attempted to quell the doubts of suspicious observers by placing time, place and manner restrictions on the policies governing the meetings of student religious clubs. For example, it required that all meetings must be voluntary and student-initiated; prohibited the use of administrative, faculty or outside sponsors; and limited the conditions under which an outside speaker could attend.[50]

Over the course of the following year, the Hatfield/Bonker proposal enlisted a broad base of support, both inside and outside the religious community. Among the supporters of the Religious Speech Protection Act were many of the established mainline Protestant lobbies, which traditionally had been staunchly separationist on issues raising problems of religious establishment, especially when they involved the public school system. In addition, many Democrats in both the House and Senate who had raised objections to the proposed school prayer amendments earlier that spring, were, by the summer, offering enthusiastic support for the "equal access" legislation. Democratic support of the proposal was no doubt partially a result of election-year politics. Having witnessed the resurgence in religious political activism that accompanied the election of Ronald Reagan to the White House and Republican takeover in the Senate, few Democratic legislators wanted to get caught on the wrong side of an issue that enjoyed considerable support in the mainline and New Right religious communities. Many Democratic legislators had lost their seats in 1980 because they were portrayed as "out-of-touch" with mainstream American social values. For those who wanted to retain their seats and avoid another round of attacks, support for equal access legislation was viewed by many as a politically wise choice.

Seeing no chance to derail the legislative momentum that had manifested itself in support of the Hatfield/Bonker bill, Representative Don Edwards (D-CA) introduced separate legislation, "The Secondary School Equality of Access Act." The Edwards bill included language that also authorized schools to grant access to student clubs designed to further "political and philosophical goals," and included stricter implementation guidelines. Representative Edwards originally had been one of the more outspoken opponents of equal access legislation; but, given the certainty that Congress would pass some version of an equal access bill, Edwards decided to soften the blow by forcing compromise on some of its key features.

Finally, in July 1984, Congress enacted what was finally called the Equal Access Act. It passed the Senate by a vote of 88-11 and the House by a 337-77 margin, and was signed into law by President Reagan in early August. In its final form, the Equal Access Act incorporated most of the major provisions of the Hatfield/Bonker and Edwards bills, plus additional guidelines crafted primarily by religious and civil liberties separationist organizations. Among its more important features, the final Equal Access Act included language that specified the circumstances under which schools were required to permit student religious clubs the use of their facilities. If a school permitted one noncurriculum-related club to meet on campus, it had created a "limited open forum" which then required it to accommodate all noncurriculum groups that wanted access to its facilities, including religious clubs. The final language of the Equal Access Act provided an important clarification of the terms which public schools were obligated to follow in permitting noncurriculum clubs to conduct meetings on campus. According to the final version, if a public secondary school has not created an open forum, it is not bound by the Equal Access Act to accommodate student religious clubs.

On the other hand, Congress created a wide opening to ensure that, under most circumstances, student religious organizations could meet in public schools through the loose statutory construction of the Equal Access Act. Even more ominous is the possibility that public schools will lose their traditional discretion over the student clubs entitled to official recognition and commensurate privileges, since the conditions permitting access for student clubs to their facilities carry over to all clubs without regard to religious, political or philosophical content. This leaves open the possibility that student groups promoting racial and religious extremism must be accorded the same treatment as other student clubs, turning a decision that once rested in the hands of school administrators into a problematic First Amendment question for the courts to decide.

The Court may not have intended to turn the nation's public schools into franchises of London's Hyde Park, but it is a scenario made more likely as a result of Justice O'Connor's analysis in *Westside v. Mergens (1990)* upholding the constitutionality and statutory construction of the Equal Access Act. Justice O'Connor acknowledged that school administrators would have to monitor carefully the religious activities of student groups meeting on campus and exercise discretion when deciding to permit other clubs access to their facilities in order to ensure compliance with the Act. [51] This degree of monitoring results in a relationship between government and individual that contravenes constitutional principles fundamental to the meaning of the free speech and establishment clauses of the First Amendment.

The Equal Access Act still has its share of critics, both within and outside the coalition of religious and secular organizations that opposed it. *The New York Times* referred to the Equal Access Act as an "atrocity" in an editorial it ran shortly after Congress passed the legislation. [52] *The Washington Post*, which had published no less than six editorials calling for Congress to defeat the Equal Access Act during the lawmaking stage of the bill, greeted the final version of the Act with skepticism and despair, [53] and expressed disappointment with the outcome in *Mergens*. [54]

To the religious and secular organizations that had fought vigorously for years at the state and federal levels, in both the judicial and legislative branches, to protect the historic Supreme Court decisions removing the vestiges of sectarian influence in public institutions, the enactment of the Equal Access Act represented not only a major legislative defeat, but an indication that a more accommodationist view of the relationship between religion and civil government was not confined to the changing jurisprudence of the Supreme Court. For church-state separationists, the message of the Equal Access Act is quite clear; its ultimate goal is to circumvent the school prayer decisions of the Supreme Court and promote religious activities in the public schools. Federal legislation protecting the right of student religious clubs to use public school facilities does not embody the power and scope of a constitutional amendment, but it is the next best thing. The legislation was greeted cautiously and guardedly by many organizations, especially the Jewish congregational and civil rights groups, which view equal access as a pungent reminder of their minority status.

Now that Congress has shown that it is willing acquiesce to religious accommodationists in the area of religion and the public schools, traditionally the most delicate and politically divisive area of church-state relations, fear abounds that the federal government will seek to provide even greater assistance to the desires of majoritarian religious interests. The Equal Access Act also signaled to state legislatures that they are now free to write concurrent legislation tailoring equal access rules to their own particular needs. For the first time, Congress has placed the imprimatur of the federal government on religious activities in the public schools.

Conclusion

In his famous *Memorial and Remonstrance Against Religious Assessments*, first published in 1784, James Madison passionately argued against the taxation of Virginians to support the establishment of an official church because it forced a citizen to violate the dictates of his or her conscience. Moreover, he wrote that "the same authority which can force a citizen to contribute three pence only of his property for the support of any one establishment, *may force him to conform to any other establishment in all cases.*" [55] Embodied in that view is the idea that religion is an intimate and private relationship between the individual and the spiritual world. Madison believed that a society of linear progress was bound to respect the importance of religion as a moral and ordering force in the civil polity, but to ensure the sanctity of religion it was necessary to sever it from political authority.

Although the First Amendment has survived over two centuries of assault on the separationist principles first articulated by Madison and Jefferson in the early years of the Republic, the church-state decisions of the Court during the last decade now cast a considerable shadow on the future of that heritage. The Court, traditionally and strongly countermajoritarian in its treatment of the First Amendment religion clauses, has assumed a new role in the separation of powers that places respect for the will of legislative majorities above the vigorous protection of the rights of religious minorities. The Court has stopped short of ignoring its constitutional obligation to prohibit the political branches from establishing religion in our public life, but it has shown much greater tolerance in allowing government to pursue legislative goals that respect establishments of religion in all facets of our public life. A subtle distinction, perhaps, but an important one nonetheless.

Contemporary America finds itself preparing to reconsider the traditional alignment of constitutional values and social forces that are bound together to shape the modern consensus on the relationship between religion and the state as it enters the 1990s. It leaves behind an era in which pressure from religious conservatives to encourage greater government accommodation and support for religion ascended to unprecedented levels. At the same time, ironically, constitutional doctrine protecting religious free exercise, especially for nontraditional observers, underwent a drastic curtailment. The heightened level of religious political activism in the 1980s by once dormant evangelical and fundamentalist religious communities, the rise of a church-state jurisprudence in the Supreme Court less sensitive to religious minorities, and a receptive climate in Congress and the state legislatures to provide legislative support for religion in the public domain all combined to make the decade a revolutionary period for religious politics.

[1] Alexis de Tocqueville, *Democracy in America* 295 (J.P. Mayer, ed. 1969).

[2] Id. at 298.

[3] *Abington v. Schempp*, 374 U.S. 203 (1963); and *Engel v. Vitale*, 370 U.S. 421 (1962).

[4] *E.g., Aguilar v. Felton*, 473 U.S. 402 (1985); *Grand Rapids v. Ball*, 473 U.S. 373; *PEARL v. Regan*, 444 U.S. 646 (1980); *PEARL v. Nyquist*, 413 U.S. 756 (1973); *Lemon v. Kurtzman*, 403 U.S. 602 (1971).

[5] *Edwards v. Aguillard*, 482 U.S. 578 (1987); *Epperson v. Arkansas*, 393 U.S. 421 (1968).

[6] *Torcaso v. Watkins*, 367 U.S. 488 (1961).

[7] *E.g., United States v. Sisson*, 399 U.S. 267 (1970); *Welsh v. United States*, 398 U.S. 333 (1970); *United States v. Seeger*, 380 U.S. 163 (1965).

[8] *E.g., Frazee v. Illinois Department of Employment Security*, 489 U.S. 829, 109 S. Ct. 1514 (1989); *Hobbie v. Employment Commission*, 480 U.S. 136 (1987); *Ansonia v. Philbrook*, 499 U.S. 60 (1986); *Thomas v. Review Board*, 450 U.S. 772 (1981); *Sherbert v. Verner*, 374 U.S. 348 (1963).

[9] *Wooley v. Maynard*, 430 U.S. 705 (1977); and *Wisconsin v. Yoder*, 406 U.S. 205 (1972).

[10] *County of Allegheny v. American Civil Liberties Union*, 109 S. Ct. 3086 (1989); *McCreary v. Stone*, 739 F. 2d 716 (2d Cir. 1984), *aff'd by an equally divided Court, sub nom Scarsdale v. McCreary*, 471 U.S. 83 (1985); *Lynch v. Donnelly*, 465 U.S. 668 (1984).

[11] *Mueller v. Allen*, 463 U.S. 388 (1983).

[12] *Marsh v. Chambers*, 463 U.S. 753 (1983).

[13] *Board of Education of Westside Community Schools v. Mergens*, 110 S. Ct. 2356 (1990).

[14] *Widmar v. Vincent*, 454 U.S. 263 (1981).

[15] *Bowen v. Kendrick*, 487 U.S. 589 108 S. Ct. 2562 (1988).

[16] *Edwards v. Aguillard*, 482 U.S. 578 (1987).

[17] *Wallace v. Jaffree*, 472 U.S. 38 (1985).

[18] *See Wallace v. Jaffree*, 472 U.S. at 71, 73, 74-76, (Justice O'Connor, concurring) ("The *Engel* and *Abington* decisions are not dispositive on the constitutionality of moment of silence laws... By mandating a moment of silence, a State does not necessarily endorse any activity that might occur during the period... In determining whether the government intends a moment of silence statute to convey a message of endorsement or disapproval of religion, a court has no license to psychoanalyze legislators. If a legislature expresses a plausible secular purpose for a moment of silence statute in either the text or the legislative history, or if the statute disclaims an intent to encourage prayer over alternatives during a moment of silence, then courts should generally defer to that stated intent... The relevant issue is whether an objective observer, acquainted with the text, legislative history, and implementation of a statute, would perceive it as a state endorsement of prayer in public schools. A moment of silence law that is clearly drafted and implemented so as to permit prayer, meditation, and reflection within the prescribed period, without endorsing one alternative over the others, should pass this test."). *See also Aguillard*, 482 U.S. at 605, (Justice Powell, concurring) ("Even though I find Louisiana's Balanced Treatment Act unconstitutional, I adhere to the view that the States and locally elected school boards should have the responsibility for determining the educational policy of the public schools. A decision respecting the subject matter to be taught in public schools does not violate the Establishment Clause simply because the material to be taught happens to coincide or harmonize with the tenets of some or all religions.").

19 *Lynch v. Donnelly*, at 465 U.S. 668, 672-73 (emphasis added).

20 *Goldman v. Weinberger*, 475 U.S. 503 (1986).

21 *Lyng v. Northwest Indian Cemetery Protective Association*, 485 U.S. 439 (1988).

22 *Bowen v. Roy*, 476 U.S. 693 (1986); and *United States v. Lee*, 455 U.S. 252 (1982).

23 *Heffron v. International Society for Krishna Consciousness*, 452 U.S. 640 (1981).

24 *Employment Division, Dept. of Human Resources of Oregon v. Smith*, 110 S. Ct. 1595 (1990).

25 403 U.S. 602 (1971).

26 Id. at 612-13.

27 Further encouragement for the Supreme Court to discard *Lemon* has come from the U.S. Department of Justice, which has submitted an *amicus curiae* brief in a case now pending review by the Supreme Court. In *Weisman v. Lee*, 908 F.2d 1090 (1st Cir. 1990), *cert. granted*, 111 S. Ct. 1305 (1991) (No. 90-1014), in which the First Circuit Court of Appeals ruled that invocations and benedictions given during junior high and high school commencement exercises violated the establishment clause, the Justice Department has asked the Court to accept the case in order to "reconsider the scope and application" of the *Lemon* test in establishment clause cases. *See* Brief of the United States at 14, *amicus curiae, Lee v. Weisman, on petition for certiorari*. The Justice Department has argued that the *Lemon* test should be replaced with a less rigorous standard that would permit the "accommodation of religious heritage in civic life," id. at 15, and other government-sponsored religious practices that are "not coercive and not part of an establishment of an official church," id. at 16.

28 *See Marsh*, 463 U.S. at 796, (Justice Brennan, dissenting) ("The Court makes no pretense of subjecting Nebraska's practice of legislative prayer to any of the formal 'tests' that have traditionally structured our inquiry under the Establishment Clause. That it fails to do so is, in a sense, a good thing, for it simply confirms that the Court is carving out an exception to the Establishment Clause rather than reshaping Establishment Clause doctrine to accommodate legislative prayer.").

29 *See, e.g., Allegheny*, 109 S. Ct. at 3134, (Justice Kennedy, dissenting) ("I am content for present purposes to remain within the *Lemon* framework, but do not wish to be seen as advocating, let alone adopting, that test as our primary guide in this difficult area. Persuasive criticism of *Lemon* has emerged. Our cases often question its utility in providing concrete answers to Establishment Clause questions. . . . Substantial revision of our Establishment Clause doctrine may be in order."); *Wallace v. Jaffree*, 472 U.S. 38, 110 (1985) (Justice Rehnquist, dissenting) ("The [*Lemon*] three-part test represents a determined effort to craft a workable rule from an historically faulty doctrine; but the rule can only be as sound as the doctrine it attempts to service. The three-part test has simply not provided adequate standards for deciding Establishment Clause cases, as this Court has slowly come to realize. . . . The true meaning of the Establishment Clause can only be seen in its history."); *Lynch*, 465 U.S. at 688-89, (Justice O'Connor, concurring) ("Our prior cases have used the three-part test articulated in *Lemon v. Kurtzman*, [citations omitted], as a guide to detecting these two forms of unconstitutional government action. It has never been entirely clear, however, how the three parts of the test relate to the principles enshrined in the Establishment Clause. Focusing on institutional entanglement and on endorsement or disapproval of religion clarifies the *Lemon* test as an analytical device.").

30 *See Lynch*, 465 U.S. at 689 (Justice O'Connor, concurring).

31 Id.

[32] The prominent liberal constitutional scholar and Harvard Law School Professor Laurence Tribe has given high marks to Justice O'Connor's development of the "endorsement" standard to replace *Lemon* in analyzing establishment clause cases, calling her "religion test the best effort around." *See Sandra Day O'Connor Emerges as Key Player in High Court Rulings*, The Wall Street Journal, June 1, 1990.

[33] 110 S. Ct. 2356 (1990).

[34] Equal Access Act of 1984, 98 Stat. 1302, 20 U.S.C. 4071-74.

[35] *See Mergens*, 110 S. Ct. at 2370-73.

[36] 472 U.S. 38, 110 (1985) (Justice Rehnquist, dissenting) ("The Framers intended the Establishment Clause to prohibit the designation of any church as a "national" one. The Clause was also designed to stop the Federal Government from asserting a preference for one religious denomination or sect over others . . . however, nothing in the Establishment Clause requires government to be strictly neutral between religion and irreligion, nor does that Clause prohibit Congress or the States from pursuing legitimate secular ends through nondiscriminatory sectarian means.")

[37] *See Allegheny*, 109 S. Ct. at 3146 (Justice Kennedy, dissenting, joined by Chief Justice Rehnquist, and Justices Scalia and White ("Our role is enforcement of a written Constitution. In my view, the principles of the Establishment Clause and our Nation's historic traditions of diversity and pluralism allow communities to make reasonable judgments respecting the accommodation or acknowledgement of holidays with both cultural and religious aspects. No constitutional violation occurs when they do so by displaying a symbol of the holiday's religious origins.").

[38] 310 U.S. 296 (1940).

[39] 330 U.S. 1 (1947).

[40] *See* Gregg Ivers, *Organized Religion and the Supreme Court*, 32 Journal of Church and State 775-93 (1990); Frank J. Sorauf, *The Wall of Separation* (1976); Richard E. Morgan, *The Politics of Religious Conflict* (1968).

[41] *See* Matthew C. Moen, *The Christian Right and Congress* (1989); Allen D. Hertzke, *Representing God in Washington* (1988); and A. James Reichley, *Religion in American Public Life* (1985).

[42] The Adolescent Family Life Act of 1981, 95 Stat. 578, 42 U.S.C. 300(z), *et. seq.*

[43] The Adolescent Health Services and Pregnancy Prevention Act of 1978, 92 Stat. 3595-3601.

[44] *See Kendrick*, 108 S. Ct. at 2571-79.

[45] Id. at 2582 (Justice Blackmun, dissenting).

[46] For further discussion of the interplay between the Reagan Administration and the conservative religious lobbies on the school prayer debates of 1983-84, *see* Moen, *Christian Right and Congress*, 113-20; Hertzke, *Representing God in Washington*, 165- 67.

[47] *Abington v. Schempp*, 374 U.S. 203 (1963); *Engel v. Vitale*, 370 U.S. 421 (1962).

[48] 454 U.S. 263 (1981).

[49] Discussion of the legislative struggle over the Equal Access Act of 1984 is taken from Moen, *Christian Right and Congress*; Hertzke, *Representing God in Washington*.

[50] Equal Access Act of 1984, 98 Stat. 1302-03.

[51] *Mergens*, 110 S. Ct. at 2373.

[52] *School Prayer Windfalls*, The New York Times, August 1, 1984.

[53] *The Unequal Access Bill*, The Washington Post, April 16, 1984; *The Unequal Access Bill*, The Washington Post, April 13, 1984; *End Run on Religion in Schools*, The Washington Post, May 11, 1984; *Prayer Meetings in School*, The Washington Post, May 15, 1984; *Equal Access Revised*, The Washington Post, July 25, 1984; *Insult, Injury and School Prayer*," The Washington Post, July 30, 1984.

[54] *Religious Meetings in Schools*, The Washington Post, June 6, 1990.

[55] James Madison, *Memorial and Remonstrance Against Religious Assessments*, June 20, 1785.

CHAPTER TWO

RELIGION AND THE PUBLIC SCHOOLS

Proponents of religious accommodation in our public life have generally viewed with contempt the decisions of the Supreme Court in *Engel v. Vitale (1962)*[1] and *Abington v. Schempp (1963)*,[2] which outlawed state-sponsored prayer and devotional exercises in the public schools. In the accommodationist view, these historic decisions were an erroneous reading of the establishment clause by a Warren Court determined to build what Reverend Richard John Neuhaus has called a "naked public square," or a public life devoid of the moral fiber of religion.[3] Given the more receptive political and legal environment that emerged in the 1980s, it is no great surprise that conservative religious and secular interest groups made the return of state-sponsored religious practices to the public schools a leading component in their renewed drive to reshape the law of church and state. The public schoolhouse has been at the center of the debate over the meaning of the religion clauses from the dawn of the modern constitutional era; indeed, the decisions of the Court over the last four decades that have attempted to explicate the larger meaning of the establishment clause have, with some notable exceptions,[4] often turned on the constitutional limits of sectarian influence in public education and government financial assistance to religious schools.

State and federal legislation enacted during the decade to permit public schools the right to integrate religious doctrine, religious practices and student religion clubs into their educational mission, most of which ran counter to the settled establishment clause doctrine of the Court, reflected the new wave of religious revivalism sweeping the country and the emerging political force behind it. Instrumental in bringing those issues before the legislatures and the courts were organizations whose support came from religious evangelicals and fundamentalists determined to redefine the contours of establishment clause law. These organizations acquired a new political sophistication in the intervening years between the end of the Warren Court era and the election of Ronald Reagan, and now they understand how to pull the levers of American politics to their advantage.[5]

In a reprisal of the arguments that greeted its landmark decisions a generation before, the Court again found itself caught in the middle of a political crossfire between competing visions of the proper place of religion in the public schools. It faced the unenviable task of trying to resolve through constitutional adjudication what the legislative process could not—the limit the Constitution places on religion as a moral and pedagogical component in the public school system. The debate centered on three areas: religious doctrine, equal access and curriculum reform.

Religious Doctrine

At the outset of its 1980 Term, the Supreme Court issued its first definitive ruling in over a decade on the constitutionality of state-endorsed religious texts and materials in the public schools. In *Stone v. Graham (1980)*,[6] the Court ruled that a Kentucky statute directing state elementary and secondary public schools to post a copy of the Ten Commandments in their classrooms violated the First Amendment. The Court, in a 5-4 *per curiam* opinion, reversed the decision of a Kentucky trial court, sustained on appeal to the state supreme court, that found the statute to have the secular purpose of advancing a historical and literary understanding of the Bible.

Using the tripartite *Lemon* test, the Court found that the Kentucky law was devoid of a secular purpose. Relying on its landmark decision in *Schempp*, which struck down the recitation of Biblical scripture and verse in the public schools, the Court in *Stone* held that

> the preeminent purpose for posting the Ten Commandments on schoolroom walls is plainly religious in nature. The Ten Commandments is undeniably a sacred text in the Jewish and Christian faiths, and no legislative recitation of a supposed secular purpose can blind us to that fact.... This is not a case in which the Ten Commandments are integrated into the school curriculum, where the Bible may constitutionally be used in an appropriate study of history, civilization, ethics, comparative religion, or the like. Posting of religious texts on the wall serves no such educational purpose.[7]

The opinion of the Court in *Stone* reaffirmed the separationist principles articulated in the historic *Schempp* and *Engel* decisions. A more problematic question that, surprisingly, had failed to reach the Court in the ensuing period was the constitutionality of silent prayer laws permitting teachers to set aside time for student worship but, in contrast to *Engel* did not involve the state's hand in determining the content of classroom devotionals. Five years later, in *Wallace v. Jaffree (1985)*,[8] the Court finally confronted that long-anticipated First Amendment issue.

The Alabama state legislature enacted a trilogy of statutes from 1978 to 1982 that authorized public school authorities to provide a moment of silence at the beginning of each school day for student meditation, reflection or prayer. The first law, passed in 1978, required elementary school teachers to provide a minute of silence "for meditation" before the first morning class.[9] In 1981, the legislature enacted a second statute that authorized elementary and secondary school teachers to provide "a period of silence not to exceed one minute in duration . . . for meditation or voluntary prayer."[10] One year later, Alabama passed the most comprehensive of its three back-to-back legislative attempts aimed at restoring school prayer. The 1982 Alabama statute gave "any teacher or professor" in any public educational institution within the state of Alabama the right to lead "willing students" in specifically worded prayer that expressly recognized "Almighty God. . .Creator and Supreme Judge of the World." [11]

On May 28, 1982 Ishmael Jaffree, an attorney and resident of Mobile County, Alabama, filed a complaint on behalf of his three children against the Mobile County School Board, school officials and the teachers of his three children seeking a declaratory judgment and restraining order against the religious practices sanctioned by the county school system. Jaffree further alleged that two of his children had been coerced into participating in school religious exercises and subjected to repeated attempts at religious indoctrination, and that numerous private attempts on his part to stop the religious observances had failed. Finally, he argued that the presence of ongoing religious practices in the public schools, maintained with the full support of the school board, violated the First and Fourteenth Amendments to the United States Constitution. Jaffree did not, however, specifically refer to any of the Alabama prayer statutes.

Less than a week later, Jaffree filed an amended complaint specifically challenging the constitutionality of the Alabama prayer laws. At an evidentiary hearing held in federal district court to consider Jaffree's motion for an injunction, State Senator Donald G. Holmes, the leading sponsor of the 1981 bill, testified that the purpose of the statute was to "return voluntary prayer to our public schools. . .it is a beginning and a step in the right direction. . .*with no other purpose in mind*." [12]

Shortly thereafter the court issued a preliminary injunction ruling that Jaffree would likely prevail on the merits of his complaint because none of the Alabama prayer statutes, and in particular the 1981 and 1982 laws, reflected a secular legislative purpose. However, in November 1982, after a full trial, Judge Brevard Hand, who had just issued the order enjoining the state school system from continuing religious practices, then issued a startling opinion reversing his earlier injunction on the grounds that the Alabama prayer statutes did not violate the First Amendment because the establishment clause did not apply to the states. After a lengthy view of what he called newly uncovered historical evidence, Judge Hand wrote that the "Establishment Clause of the First Amendment to the United States Constitution does not prohibit the state from establishing a religion." [13] According to Judge Hand, the ban against government establishment of religion applied only to the national government.

Not surprisingly, the Eleventh Circuit Court of Appeals reversed the decision of Judge Hand. The Eleventh Circuit did not consider the constitutional challenge to the 1978 statute that permitted teachers to allow a period of silence "for meditation," but it did find the 1981 and 1982 laws "to advance and encourage religious activity." [14] An appeal from the state for a rehearing *en banc* was denied, but drew the dissent of four judges who argued that the court should have agreed to review the constitutionality of the 1981 statute authorizing moments-of-silence for "meditation or voluntary prayer." The Supreme Court considered the disagreement among the Eleventh Circuit judges important enough to accept *Wallace v. Jaffree* for review during the 1984-85 Term, limiting the question for decision to the constitutionality of that provision of the statute.

In a 6-3 decision, the Supreme Court found the 1981 Alabama statute to violate the purpose prong of the Lemon test. Justice John Paul Stevens' opinion relied extensively on the legislative history surrounding the enactment of the statute, holding that the Alabama state legislature enacted it for the sole purpose of expressing the State's endorsement of prayer activities for one minute at the beginning of each school day. The addition of 'or voluntary prayer' [to the 1978 law] indicates that the State intended to characterize prayer as a favored practice. Such an endorsement is not consistent with the established principle that the Government must pursue a course of complete neutrality towards religion. [15]

Jaffree reassured nervous separationists that the decisions from *Engel* through *Stone* outlawing state-prescribed or endorsed religious observances still retained their constitutional backbone against new challenges. Furthermore, the open dismissal by the Supreme Court of Judge Hand's trial court decision holding the constitutional command of the establishment clause to mean that only the federal government was barred from establishing or supporting an official state church reaffirmed the separationist principles embodied in the Jeffersonian-Madison vision of the relationship between government and religion. However, the *Jaffree* Court did not address the issue of whether the establishment clause prohibited a "moment of silence" *per se*. In her concurring opinion, Justice Sandra Day O'Connor wrote that a moment-of-silence law "drafted and implemented so as to permit prayer, meditation and reflection. . .without endorsing one alternative over the others," would comport with her reading of the establishment clause, a view that Justice Lewis Powell also endorsed. [16]

Far from extinguishing the school prayer debate, the *Jaffree* opinion offered puzzled legislatures a murky set of guidelines governing future efforts to write constitutional school prayer legislation. Statutes allowing verbal religious exercises to take place under the direction of school officials or allowing administrators control over the content of students' devotionals remained unconstitutional; [17] "pure" moment-of-silence laws that lacked a legislative record documenting a religious purpose in their enactment *appeared* to have the constitutional blessing of the Court. In fact, Justice O'Connor's *Jaffree* concurrence is all but a blueprint for legislatures wishing to enact moment-of-silence statutes. Nonetheless, the Court refused to clarify that aspect of its holding in *Jaffree* when given the chance two years later in *May v. Cooperman* (1987). [18]

The issue in *Cooperman* centered on the constitutionality of a New Jersey statute that set aside a moment-of-silence in the public schools "for quiet and private contemplation or introspection" [19] originally passed in 1982 over the veto of Governor Thomas P. Kean. Several public school students, their parents and a New Jersey public high school teacher mounted a constitutional challenge to the statute in federal district court almost immediately after it was passed. The New Jersey Attorney General refused to defend the statute in court, calling it a thinly veiled attempt by the legislature to reintroduce prayer in the public school system. Determined to press the matter, the state legislature subsequently hired outside counsel.

In October 1983, District Judge Dickinson R. Debevoise ruled that the New Jersey moment-of-silence statute violated all three prongs of the *Lemon* test. First, the district court found the statute to have a religious purpose—"to mandate that all students assume the posture of one traditional form of prayer." [20] Second, it found the law to have the dual effect of advancing and inhibiting religion, a departure from settled establishment clause analysis under *Lemon*, which generally focuses on whether the statute has advanced or inhibited religion, but not whether it has resulted in both outcomes. Judge Debevoise found the statute advanced religion by designating "a time and place when children and teachers may pray if they do so in a particular manner." The statute inhibited religion because the mandated prayer drained the vitality of other students' religious observances.[21] Finally, the district court found the statute to foster excessive entanglement between religion and government because it promoted divisiveness among religious and nonreligious groups that threatened the order of the daily school agenda.[22]

On appeal, the Court of Appeals for the Third Circuit affirmed the lower court decision that the New Jersey law lacked any secular purpose, but it disagreed with Judge Debevoise's interpretation of the statute under the *Lemon* test. Instead, the Third Circuit ruled that the effect and entanglement provisions of the *Lemon* test were designed to analyze whether the statute resulted in neutrality towards religion. Nonetheless, the Third Circuit's conclusion that the law lacked any secular purpose was sufficient to sustain Judge Debevoise's decision. The Third Circuit followed the reasoning of the Supreme Court's *Jaffree* holding to reach its decision in *Cooperman*. In reviewing the legislative record, the Third Circuit found the law rooted in a clear religious purpose. It incorporated no direct reference to religion in its text, but the court, following the guidelines laid down in *Jaffree*, struck down the moment-of-silence statute on the grounds that the legislative record was replete with evidence of the religious purpose behind the bill. The Supreme Court granted *certiorari* and heard oral argument to decide the merits of the establishment clause issue in *Cooperman*, but it declined to reach the issue in its opinion, which dismissed the appeal because the plaintiffs lacked standing.

Clearly, *Jaffree* and *Cooperman* are the two most important cases elucidating the constitutional limitations on state-sponsored religious devotionals in the public schools since the landmark decisions of *Engel* and *Schempp* over twenty-five years ago. Unfortunately, the failure of the Supreme Court to reach the constitutional question in *Cooperman* means that a large element of uncertainty currently exists in how it and other courts will view the legislative purpose behind the enactment of facially neutral moment-of-silence statutes challenged in future litigation. If the Court relies on *Jaffree* and continues to scrutinize the legislative histories of similar laws, a chance exists that it will continue to consider *Jaffree* controlling under those circumstances. However, if the *Jaffree* concurrences of Justices Powell and O'Connor, both of whom indicated that "some moment-of-silence statutes may be constitutional,"[23] assume a more central place in the approach of the Court to subsequent school prayer cases, the future suggests an outcome quite different from the present state of the law. Constitutional challenges to *Jaffree* and attempts to sustain "pure" moment-of-silence statutes could succeed or fail depending upon whether the religious purpose driving the enactment of such laws are appropriately camouflaged in the legislative record and the extent to which the conservative wing of the Court finds legislative history a relevant guide in interpreting such statutes.

Equal Access

The tension inherent in attempting to reconcile the constitutional promises of the establishment, free exercise and free speech clauses of the First Amendment is nowhere better illustrated than in the debate over equal access for student religious clubs in the public schools. Prior to the enactment of the Equal Access Act of 1984,[24] the Supreme Court, in *Widmar v. Vincent (1981)*,[25] had ruled that once public universities made their campus facilities available for noncurriculum student clubs, they created an "open forum" accessible to all groups regardless of their stated purpose or activities. *Widmar* grew out of a challenge to a University of Missouri Board of Regents regulation that prohibited the use of "university buildings or grounds . . . for purposes of religious worship or religious teaching." [26] The university argued that it was obligated under the Missouri Constitution and the establishment clause of the federal Constitution to prohibit student religious clubs from using its facilities.

Conversely, the student religious club, which consisted of evangelical Christians whose stated purpose was to meet for prayer, hyms, Bible commentary and discussion of religious views and experience, [27] brought suit against the university, alleging that the regulation violated the free exercise and free speech clauses of the First Amendment. The students argued that the establishment clause had no bearing on the case; rather, the issue was state-imposed discrimination against student religious clubs based upon their content and purpose—a free speech issue. Furthermore, the students argued that universities, by their very definition, emboldened the enterprise of intellectual pluralism that considered access to the marketplace of ideas as fundamental in the development of an enlightened and educated public discourse.

The U.S. District Court for the Western District of Missouri ruled that the establishment clause forbade the use of state facilities by student religious groups for the purposes of worship and Bible study. It did not reach the free speech arguments offered by the students in support of their right to equal access. On appeal, the Eighth Circuit Court of Appeals reversed, holding that religious speech falls within the protection of the speech clause of the First Amendment. It also ruled that the University of Missouri, in allowing student groups to use its buildings, had created an "open forum" and therefore could not target religious groups for exclusion. In rejecting the district court's conclusion that student-initiated religious worship or teaching on campus would impermissibly advance religion in contravention of the establishment clause, the Eighth Circuit instead found that allowing student religious clubs access to campus had "the primary effect of advancing the university's admittedly secular purpose—to develop students' social and cultural awareness as well as their intellectual curiosity." [28]

The Supreme Court, in an 8-1 opinion written by Justice Powell, affirmed the decision of the Eighth Circuit. Agreeing with the appellate court finding that the free speech clause controlled the constitutional questions presented in *Widmar*, the Court held the university regulation to have the impermissible discriminatory effect of barring student religious clubs from what was clearly an otherwise "open forum." [29] The Court flatly rejected the university's establishment clause argument that religion stood to benefit from an equal access policy which included religious clubs among those eligible for use of campus facilities. In two major respects, the Court found the benefits that accrued to religion incidental. First, the "open forum" policy of the university did not constitute state endorsement or advancement of religion. [30] Second, the multiplicity of student clubs, both secular and religious, would be sufficiently diverse to preclude any prospect that religious organizations would dominate campus life. [31]

In an important footnote, the Court reiterated its long-standing view that college students are less impressionable than their "younger, secondary school" counterparts and more capable of treating religious speech as but one component of the intellectual environment associated with academic life. A college setting, the Court reasoned, diminished the likelihood that student-initiated religious clubs would become a coercive force in campus life, a problem that had long concerned the Court at the high school level. [32] Given the strong line that the Court had taken against state support for religious exercises in the public schools, even separationists for the most part accepted the distinction between high school and college students outlined in Justice Powell's opinion, and remained reasonably assured that equal access would not find its way to the high school level. But the decision of the Supreme Court upholding the Equal Access Act in *Westside v. Mergens (1990)* [33] eviscerates that long-standing distinction and opens the door for an even greater place for religion in the public schools.

Mergens also marked the first time that a federal appellate court ruled on whether the Equal Access Act violated the establishment clause. The Eighth Circuit Court of Appeals and the Supreme Court gave the constitutional arguments little more than cursory review in their opinions. Each court centered their analysis on the statutory construction of the Act and whether it applied to the facts of the case. Nonetheless, each appellate ruling dismissed the establishment clause challenges to the Act. Prior to *Mergens*, the lower federal courts generally had declined to extend *Widmar* to student equal access claims in elementary and secondary public schools, [34] although there had been a few exceptions. [35] Given the importance that *Mergens* will have in redefining the law permitting equal access for religious clubs in the public schools, it is important to review the legal evolution of the equal access issue in the federal courts.

In two cases decided prior to the passage of the Equal Access Act, *Nartowicz v. Clayton County (1984)* [36] and *Lubbock Civil Liberties Union v. Lubbock Independent School District (1983)*, [37] federal appellate courts struck down equal access policies in two different states as violative of the establishment clause. Both cases involved the right of student groups to meet on school property before or after class hours. In each case, these religious clubs held prayer meetings and spiritual consultations, which had not only received school board approval, but endorsement as well.

Since 1971, the Lubbock County School District had allowed classroom prayers led by teachers, morning Bible readings followed by a minute of silence announced over the school intercom system, distribution of the Christian Bible to fifth and sixth grade children by the Gideon Camp, and school assemblies featuring Christian evangelical speakers. Despite a complaint filed by the Lubbock Civil Liberties Union ("LCLU") later that year to enjoin these school-sponsored religious practices, they continued to take place over the next eight years. In 1980, the LCLU filed suit in federal district court seeking a constitutional ruling on the policy of the Lubbock school board. At that point, the school amended its policies to require that students and not teachers were to initiate all religious activities and exercises conducted under school auspices. Nonetheless, the LCLU continued to challenge the Lubbock policies as violative of the establishment clause, arguing that the religious exercises questioned prior to the amendment would still be authorized. The lawsuit focused on the following provision:

> The School Board permits students to gather at the school with super-vision either before or after regular school hours on the same basis as other groups as determined by the school administration to meet for any educational, moral, religious or ethical purposes so long as attendance at such meetings is voluntary. [38]

In deciding the case, the U.S. District Court for the Northern District of Texas found the pre-1980 religious activities unconstitutional, but upheld the facial validity of the 1980 amendment to the school board policy. Consequently, the court refused to enter an injunction prohibiting Lubbock County from allowing state-supported religious activities to take place throughout the public school system. On appeal, the Fifth Circuit reversed the lower court's decision on the 1980 amendment. Using the *Lemon* test, it held that the Lubbock policy "implies recognition of religious activities and meetings as an integral part of the District's extracurricular program and carries with it implicit approval by school officials of those programs." [39] The Fifth Circuit also refused to accept the argument that the voluntary, student-initiated nature of the meeting nullified the establishment clause arguments, noting that the "critical factor [was] the [District's] compulsory education machinery. . .and its implicit support and approval of the religious meetings." [40]

The Fifth Circuit agreed with the lower court determination that the pre-1980 activities were unconstitutional, but it also refused to issue injunctive relief, based on its view that the practices were not likely to continue. The following year, the Lubbock School District appealed the decision to the Supreme Court, which declined to review the case.

The opinion of the Eleventh Circuit in *Nartowicz* was consistent with the Fifth Circuit's decision in *Lubbock*. *Nartowicz* involved a challenge to four distinct religious practices in the public schools that were sanctioned by the Clayton County School District, located in suburban Atlanta, Georgia. A group of parents filed suit against the school board, challenging its policy of allowing 1) religious meetings of a group called "Youth for Christ" to take place after classes; 2) voluntary school assemblies featuring speakers espousing religious doctrines; 3) signs on school property advertising the location of a church and a schedule of its religious worship services; and 4) regular announcements over the school public address system and on classroom bulletin boards advertising church and church-sponsored events. [41]

U.S. District Judge Marvin H. Shoob granted the requests of the plaintiffs and issued a preliminary injunction enjoining the school district from permitting any of these practices, holding that each one violated the establishment clause. The school district acknowledged the impropriety of the student assemblies that promoted religion as well as the placement of religious signs throughout the school, but it appealed the section of the decision that prohibited student religious clubs from meeting on school grounds and posting advertisements for church and church-sponsored events. [42]

In a brief *per curiam* opinion, the Eleventh Circuit affirmed the judgment of the lower court on both questions. The appellate court first reviewed the practice of permitting the "Youth for Christ" club to meet on school premises under faculty approval and supervision "in light of the district's apparent support of religious assemblies, religious signs and announcements of church sponsored activities via bulletin boards and public address systems," and concluded that the lower court's injunction had been proper. Turning next to the issue of school support for the announcement and advertisement of religious events, the Eleventh Circuit affirmed the lower court, holding that this practice also constituted a violation of the establishment clause because it fostered excessive entanglement between government and religion. [43]

In *Bell v. Little Axe (1985)*, [44] the Tenth Circuit Court of Appeals struck down the equal access policy of the *Little Axe* School District in Cleveland County, Oklahoma. Little Axe began when the parents of two students initiated a constitutional challenge to the Oklahoma Voluntary Prayer Act, which authorized the "board of education of each school district [to] permit those students and teachers who wish[ed] to do so to participate in voluntary prayer." [45] After the lawsuit had been initiated, the school board amended the time and manner in which the prayer sessions could be held. The new guidelines read, in part:

> All students, whether as school sponsored clubs, nonsponsored student associations or individuals shall have equal access to school facilities. . . student use of school facilities shall not be regulated on the basis of the content of the students' meetings. . . religious speech shall receive the same rights and protections as political and all other speech, including private voluntary prayer, reading from religious or political books and speaking about political or religious topics. [46]

Student prayer meetings continued to take place on school premises between 8:00 a.m., when the school buses dropped the children off at school, and 8:25 a.m., when classes began. Teachers often attended, monitored and participated in these sessions, which were advertised on classroom bulletin boards and devoted to "prayers, songs and 'testimony' concerning the benefits of knowing Jesus Christ and. . . Christianity. . . ." [47] As a result, the parents amended their lawsuit to challenge both the Little Axe School Board policies permitting student prayer meetings and the Oklahoma Prayer Act as violative of the establishment clause.

After a six-day trial, which included the testimony of expert witnesses on the religious nature of the student prayer meetings, the U.S. District Court for the Western District of Oklahoma found the prayer sessions to fail entirely the tripartite *Lemon* test. Noting that the Board provided religious services on school grounds during the school day, with teachers or school officers attending, monitoring or participating and providing governmental support, the court concluded that the sessions were of a religious nature and content and, second, that their principal or primary effect was to advance religion. [48] However the trial court found the school board policies acceptable, and did not address the constitutional considerations raised by the Oklahoma Voluntary Prayer Act because the school board had disclaimed reliance upon that law. [49]

The Tenth Circuit Court of Appeals upheld the trial court decision enjoining the school board from sponsoring student prayer meetings on school premises. It also held the "equal access" policy promulgated by the school district to be unconstitutional on the grounds that it allowed concerted religious activities to take place during the school day. [50] However, the Tenth Circuit did not decide the constitutionality of the Oklahoma prayer law for the same reasons advanced by the court below. Nonetheless, the result was a firm defeat for the Oklahoma legislature. It failed on all points to return prayer and devotional exercises to the public schools through the guise of equal access.

Less than a year later, the Seventh Circuit Court of Appeals upheld a federal district court decision in Indiana that enjoined a group of public school teachers from meeting in classrooms to pray, sing hymns and discuss the Bible before daily instruction began. In a somewhat unusual departure from previous equal access cases, the question in *May v. Evansville (1986)* [51] did not present an issue of *student* access to public school facilities, but the right of *teachers* to form religious clubs on the same premises. Mary May and several other evangelical teachers met each Tuesday morning between 7:25 and 7:45 a.m. at the Harper Elementary School in Evansville, Indiana, to engage in religious devotionals and dialogue. Subsequently barred from using school facilities upon complaints from other teachers and students, May sued the school board, its members and the superintendent of the school district seeking to lift the ban on the religious meetings. She argued in her complaint that the prohibition against faculty-initiated religious meetings violated her constitutional right to free speech.

The court first ruled out the claim that the school qualified as a public forum and dismissed the corollary argument that the teachers had a right to school facilities under the free speech clause. [52] Essential to the court's ruling was the absence of a pre-existing policy authorizing other noncurriculum clubs to meet on campus. The school had no written policy prohibiting these meetings, but they were taking place under the tacit approval of school officials. The court then proceeded to address the more important constitutional question before it—did the federal Equal Access Act provide sufficient scope to include the right of teacher-initiated religious clubs to use school facilities? The district court gave a resoundingly negative answer. It ruled in clear and convincing terms that the Act applied only to student groups; that it was intended to cover secondary rather than the elementary schools; and found no evidence that the Act even remotely provided authorization for individuals other than students to initiate religious meetings. [53] Turning to the establishment clause issue, the court ruled that for public schools to allow teacher-initiated religious clubs to meet on campus would be to take a "significant risk of creating an improper imprimatur of state approval for religious activity." [54] Finally, the court ruled that the burden of supervision placed on school administrators to monitor the religious meetings created a threat of excessive entanglement. [55]

In 1986, the Seventh Circuit Court of Appeals affirmed the lower court judgment, ruling that the free speech clause did not grant teachers a constitutional right to conduct religious meetings on campus. [56] Writing for the court, Judge Richard Posner ruled out the argument that the school had created a public forum. Thus, the decision to exclude a teacher-led prayer meeting could not be interpreted as content-based discrimination against speech. Judge Posner also distinguished private discussions from group meetings, holding that organized gatherings fall under the regulatory power of the schools in a manner that conversations do not.

The most recent pronouncement on the equal access question prior to *Mergens* came out of the Ninth Circuit in *Garnett v. Renton School District (1989)*. [57] *Garnett* stemmed from a lawsuit brought by several students from Lindbergh High School, located in the Renton School District of Washington State, contesting the policy of the school board that barred student religious groups from meeting on school premises. The purpose of the student club was to discuss the Bible and its application to contemporary student issues, and to offer members the chance to give prayer, support and encouragement to each other. Relying on *Widmar*, the students argued that their right to meet on school property was protected by the free exercise and speech clauses of the federal Constitution and similar provisions in the Washington State Constitution. Furthermore, the students argued that the Equal Access Act created an express right for student religious groups to meet in public schools.

The district court did not reach the issue of whether the Equal Access Act applied in this instance, or, as the defending parties had requested, address its constitutionality. It did rule, however, that the Washington State Constitution prohibited student religious clubs from meeting in the public schools. [58]

On appeal, the Ninth Circuit Court of Appeals affirmed the lower court decision. The Ninth Circuit agreed with the district court that granting the use of public school facilities for religious meetings violated the establishment clause. Applying the *Lemon* test, the Ninth Circuit found that equal access policies for student religious clubs whose activities encompassed evangelism and proselytization had the primary effect of advancing religion and, because the activities would require the extensive supervision of school officials, would also result in excessive entanglement. [59]

Crucial to the Ninth Circuit's decision was its dismissal of the students' free speech claim. First, the court ruled that Lindbergh High School did not qualify as a traditional public forum, [60] recognizing the traditional discretion that school officials have in controlling student access to their facilities, which includes the power to prohibit the sponsorship of student clubs, to limit political activities on campus or to regulate the content of student publications. [61] Second, the Ninth Circuit carefully delineated the constitutional protection accorded to religious expression from that given to nonreligious expression under the speech clause. It concluded on establishment clause grounds that the school board was obligated to exclude student religious clubs from access to public school facilities, or it would result in impermissible government endorsement of religion.

The parties and numerous groups filing *amicus curiae*—or "friend of the court" briefs—anticipated that *Garnett* would also force the Ninth Circuit to confront the constitutional arguments raised by the Equal Access Act. To their disappointment, the court declined to review the Act. It found the requirements of the Equal Access Act applicable to high schools whose policies on extracurricular clubs fell within the parameters of the "limited open forum" as it is defined under federal law. In the view of the Ninth Circuit, Lindbergh High School did not constitute a "traditional public forum," nor had it created a limited open forum, making the Equal Access Act inapplicable.

Still, the decision of the Ninth Circuit left both sides of the equal access controversy dissatisfied. Confusion over how to implement equal access policies continued to plague school districts caught between the conflicting commands of the federal courts, which had generally rejected lawsuits requesting the recognition of student religious clubs, and Congress, which adopted the Equal Access Act to ensure that result. Decided just one month after *Garnett*, the Eighth Circuit Court of Appeals' ruling in *Mergens* left the Supreme Court no choice but to resolve the problematic series of legal and political questions that had emerged over the Equal Access Act.

The long sequence of events leading to the Supreme Court decision in *Westside v. Mergens* began in February 1985 when Bridget Mergens, a student at Westside High School in Omaha, Nebraska, requested that the school grant formal recognition to a student-initiated Christian Bible Club and permission for the club to meet on school grounds to discuss religion and to pray. Westside had no written regulations governing the formation of student clubs, but instead required students seeking to form clubs to present their stated purposes and objectives to school officials. Upon review, school officials were empowered to decide whether proposed student clubs fell within the Westside School Board written guidelines. [62] The principal of Westside High School turned down Mergens' request. She appealed to the superintendent of the Westside Community School Board, which agreed with other school officials that recognition of a Christian Bible Club at Westside High would violate the establishment clause of the First Amendment. The School Board ruled that recognition of student religious clubs would not be consistent with Board regulations that permit only "school-sponsored, curriculum-related activities" to take place in campus buildings. [63]

Having exhausting her administrative remedies, Mergens then filed suit in federal district court alleging that the Westside School Board decision to prohibit equal access for the Christian Bible Club violated their constitutional rights of freedom of speech, freedom of assembly and association and freedom of religion guaranteed under the First and Fourteenth Amendments, and the Equal Access Act. In February 1988, the U.S. District Court for the District of Nebraska entered judgment in favor of the school board. Judge Clarence A. Beam ruled, first, that Westside High School maintained a closed forum and thus failed to trigger the Equal Access Act's applicability to the Christian Bible Club and, second, that even absent the Equal Access Act, the school did not violate the students' constitutional rights when it denied their request to use school buildings for religious meetings.

A unanimous three-judge panel for the Eighth Circuit reversed. Turning first to the statutory construction of the Equal Access Act, the court ruled that Westside High *did* maintain an open forum because it allowed noncurriculum-related student organizations access to school facilities, including the chess club and scuba diving club. The Eighth Circuit noted that Congress had not defined "noncurriculum-related" clubs in the Act, but ruled that Westside's argument that all of its student clubs were "curriculum-related" made the Equal Access Act "meaningless." [64] The Eighth Circuit also determined that the overriding purpose of the Act was to prohibit secondary public schools from making arbitrary decisions that denied access to "disfavored student club[s] based [on their] speech content . . . reaching exactly the result that Congress sought to prohibit by enacting the EAA."

On the constitutional issue, the Eighth Circuit ruled that the Equal Access Act codified the constitutional interpretation given to *Widmar*, noting that "the only difference between the EAA and *Widmar* is the EAA's express extension of the equal access principle to public secondary school students." The Eighth Circuit held that any

> constitutional attack on the EAA must therefore be predicated upon the difference between secondary school students and university students. We reject this notion because Congress considered the difference in maturity level of secondary students and university students before passing the EAA. We accept Congress' fact-finding. [65]

In conclusion, the Eighth Circuit commented that had Congress "never passed the EAA, our decision would be the same under *Widmar* alone." [66]

The Supreme Court affirmed. Writing for an 8-1 majority, Justice Sandra Day O'Connor concluded that Westside High School did maintain a "limited open forum" for noncurriculum clubs as defined by the Equal Access Act, and hence had acted counter to the intent of the Act when it denied the Christian Bible Club permission to meet on school grounds. Furthermore, Justice O'Connor rejected the arguments offered by the school board that the Equal Access Act violated the establishment clause because it would incorporate religious activities into the educational mission of Westside High School, endorse participation in student religious clubs and provide religious clubs with a state-provided platform from which to proselytize other students. Citing *Widmar* as controlling on the statutory and constitutional issues raised in *Mergens*, Justice O'Connor wrote that the Court had already concluded that equal access policies, which included "nondiscrimination against religious speech" and were applicable to qualified "open forums," did not contravene the establishment clause.[67] Thus, "the logic of *Widmar* applie[d] with equal force to the Equal Access Act."[68]

To support her conclusion, Justice O'Connor pointed to the "broad spectrum of officially recognized student clubs at Westside, and the fact that Westside students are free to initiate and organize additional student clubs," as "counteract[ing] any possible message of official endorsement or preference for religion or a particular religion."[69] The Court had found in *Widmar* that the "provision of benefits to so broad a spectrum of groups [was] an important index of secular effect."[70] The same reasoning applied in *Mergens*. Justice O'Connor also extended the *Widmar* analysis of the entanglement question to the facts raised in *Mergens*, noting that "a denial of equal access to religious speech might well create greater entanglement problems in the form of pervasive monitoring to prevent religious speech at meetings at which such speech might occur." The Equal Access Act thus survived all three prongs of the *Lemon* purpose-effect-entanglement test.

The Court also upheld the Eighth Circuit's statutory construction of the Equal Access Act. While acknowledging that "the phrase noncurriculum related student group" received no clarification from the legislative record of the Act, Justice O'Connor rejected the broad definition of "curriculum related" given to the extracurricular student groups permitted access to Westside High School facilities. "To define 'curriculum related' in a way that results in almost no schools having limited open fora," wrote Justice O'Connor, "or in a way that permits schools to evade the Act by strategically describing existing students groups, would render the Act merely hortatory."[71] Justice O'Connor concluded that Congress, when it passed the Equal Access Act, meant to include protection for all noncurriculum student clubs regardless of their content, including religious clubs.

Entering the sole dissent, Justice John Paul Stevens disagreed with both the statutory and constitutional interpretation that the majority gave the Equal Access Act. On the statutory issues, Justice Stevens wrote that the Court had construed the Act to authorize "a sweeping intrusion by the federal government into the operation of our public schools, and does so despite the absence of any indication that Congress intended to divest local school districts of their power to shape the educational environment."[72] Focusing on Justice O'Connor's interpretation of Congress' legislative purpose in permitting equal access for *all* noncurriculum clubs, Justice Stevens argued that the Court had, in a sweeping judicial stroke, ceded the traditional power of states and localities over public education to the national government without the slightest indication that that is what Congress had intended. Therefore, Justice Stevens argued,

> [i]f a high school administration continues to believe that it is sound policy to exclude controversial groups, such as political clubs, the Ku Klux Klan, and perhaps gay rights advocacy groups, from its facilities, it now must also close its doors to traditional extracurricular activities that are noncontroversial but not directly related to any course being offered at the school. Indeed, the very fact that Congress omitted any definition in the statute itself is persuasive evidence of an intent to allow local officials broad discretion in deciding whether or not to create limited public fora. I see no reason—and no evidence of congressional intent—to constrain that

discretion any more narrowly than our holding in *Widmar* requires. [73]

Noting that "we have always treated with special sensitivity the Establishment Clause problems that result when religious observances are moved into the public schools," Justice Stevens expressed displeasure with the willingness of the Court, in its desire to extend *Widmar* to the high school level, to eviscerate the distinction that the Court had long respected over the degree of religious activities permissible in secondary and higher education. [74] Justice Stevens did not express an opinion on whether the Equal Access Act violated the establishment clause. But he did criticize the majority for failing to address adequately the establishment clause questions in the case, which he maintained were "much more difficult than the majority assumes." [75] Considering the establishment clause problems that Justice O'Connor, along with Justice Marshall in his concurrence, acknowledged lurked in the background because of the coercive environment that even student-initiated religious clubs could generate under certain conditions, Justice Stevens believed the Court, like Congress, had "swept aside" real concerns in interpreting the Equal Access Act that might pose far more problematic for public schools, legislatures and the courts down the line. [76] Either way, the last word on the controversy over equal access in the public schools has not yet been spoken.

Curriculum

The revitalized legal and political debate over the treatment of religion in public school curricula is similar to the equal access cases in that the constitutional arguments supporting balanced treatment for religious doctrine in science and literature courses, like those for student religious speech, are couched in the free exercise and speech clauses of the First Amendment. But there the similarities end. Whereas the equal access cases have been confined to questions involving school endorsement or sponsorship of student-initiated religious clubs that meet after hours, the textbook and curriculum cases have raised the issue of direct support for religious doctrine as a pedagogical component in public education. Eschewing the establishment clause difficulties associated with incorporating religious doctrine into the curricula of the public schools, religious fundamentalists succeeded in resurrecting the first great public debate over the place of religion in the schools—the "Scopes" monkey trial of 1925—and returning it to the courts, albeit in a more sophisticated form.

Epperson v. Arkansas (1968), [77] the swan song of the strict separationist church-state decisions handed down by the Warren Court, struck down a 1927 Arkansas statute that prohibited the public schools from teaching "that mankind ascended or descended from a lower order of animals" or the use of textbooks that supported evolution theory. [78] Writing for a unanimous Court, Justice Abe Fortas analogized the plight of Susan Epperson, who was fired from her job as a high school biology teacher and subsequently convicted and fined under the statute by an Arkansas court, to that of John Scopes, who had suffered a similar fate in Tennessee over forty years before. [79] Justice Fortas noted that the Tennessee and Arkansas statutes were both products "of the 'fundamentalist' religious fervor of the twenties," [80] and wrote there could

be no doubt that Arkansas sought to prevent its teachers from discussing the theory of evolution because it is contrary to the belief of some that the Book of Genesis must be the exclusive source of doctrine as to the origin of man. It is clear that fundamentalist sectarian conviction was and is the law's reason for existence. [81]

Holding that the Arkansas law was "plainly" contrary to the establishment clause, *Epperson* was thought to have relegated to the constitutional dust bin anti-evolution statutes that compelled public schools to teach their students Biblical versions of human origin. Nonetheless, religious fundamentalists decided to pursue an alternative constitutional argument. Relying on theory and research advanced by a small group of scholars who argued that the study of creationism itself was a valid scientific discipline, religious fundamentalists determined to reintroduce creationism in the public school curricula decided to place the question squarely within the free speech provisions of the First Amendment. Moreover, they also argued that curriculum hostile to religion impermissibly burdened the conscience of devout students, introducing a problematic issue of religious freedom. Collapsing the arguments in a fashion reminiscent of the Jehovah's Witnesses in The *Flag Salute Cases*, [82] religious fundamentalists insisted that the First Amendment prohibits public schools from coercing schoolchildren into this cruel position of choosing between their obligations to the spiritual and secular worlds. It is an argument that federal appellate courts, including the Supreme Court, have yet to find persuasive.

Edwards v. Aguillard (1987) [83] provided a clear indication, in one of the most strongly worded church-state opinions of the 1980s, that the Court had no intention of retreating from the principles set down in *Epperson* twenty years before. The issue in *Aguillard* was the constitutionality of the 1981 Louisiana Balanced Treatment for Creation-Science and Evolution-Science Act, which prohibited public schools from teaching evolution as part of its science curriculum unless they also incorporated "creation-science." The passage of the Creationism Act represented the culmination of over ten years of work on the part of religious fundamentalists to persuade the Louisiana State Legislature that "scientific creationism" was constitutionally entitled to a place in the state science curricula under the free speech guarantees of the First Amendment. Furthermore, the Act did not prohibit or criminalize the teaching of evolution; instead, it required that "creation-science" be taught along with evolution.

In an unusual move, the Creation Science Legal Defense Fund filed a petition in federal district court immediately after the Balanced Treatment Act's passage in December 1981 seeking a declaratory judgment on its constitutionality. The Louisiana Attorney General had deputized this private organization to represent the state in subsequent litigation, fully anticipating a protracted battle in the courts. The American Civil Liberties Union filed suit the next day challenging the constitutionality of the Balanced Treatment Act, which was dismissed by the U.S. District Court for the Eastern District of Louisiana on procedural grounds. But four years later, in a separate action brought by a coalition of taxpayers, parents, teachers and religious leaders, the district court held that the Act violated the establishment clause. The Fifth Circuit Court of Appeals affirmed, noting that the intended effect of the statute was "to discredit evolution by counterbalancing its teaching at every turn with the teaching of creationism, a religious belief." [84]

The Supreme Court, voting 7-2, upheld the decision of the Fifth Circuit. Justice William Brennan, writing for the majority, appeared visibly astonished that the Louisiana State Legislature could argue that it had anything other than a religious purpose in mind when it passed the Creationism Act. According to Justice Brennan, "the preeminent purpose of the legislature was clearly to advance the religious viewpoint that a supernatural being created humankind." [85] The Court, he also noted, generally was deferential to the stated legislative purpose of a statute under review, but occasionally was required to go beyond the articulated purpose to ensure that it is "sincere and not a sham." [86] In his concurring opinion, Justice Powell found the "legislative history of the Arkansas statute prohibiting the teaching of evolution in *Epperson* strikingly similar to the legislative history of the [Louisiana] Balanced Treatment Act." [87] Justice Powell noted the similar legislative goals of the Tennessee and Louisiana legislatures, both of which "acted with the unconstitutional purpose of structuring the public school curriculum to make it compatible with a particular religious belief: 'the divine creation of man.' " [88] The legislative intent provided evidence that the act violated the purpose prong of the *Lemon* test.

Dissenting, Justice Scalia, joined by Chief Justice Rehnquist, argued that the Court had failed to respect the secular motives of the Louisiana legislature, which he believed passed the Balanced Treatment Act to promote the comprehensive teaching of the origins of human existence, not to advance fundamentalist religious doctrine. [89] He also used *Aguillard* to fire the first of several salvos calling for an abandonment of the *Lemon* test, which he argued handcuffed legislatures from taking any action that had "untoward consequences" for religion. [90] In his first major written opinion dealing with an establishment clause question, Justice Scalia attracted little support for his views, but his harsh criticism of the Court's church-state jurisprudence, which he called "embarrassing . . . and lacking in principled rationale," [91] effectively put to rest all doubts about where the new Justice would stand in future cases.

Earlier that year, in *Smith v. Board of Commissioners (1987)*, [92] the Eleventh Circuit issued a decision that ended one of the most bizarre and complex sequences of church-state litigation to come through the federal courts in years. In *Smith*, U.S. District Court Judge Brevard Hand initially ruled that 44 textbooks on the Alabama State Approved Textbook List violated the establishment clause because they promoted the "religion of secular humanism." [93] *Smith* originally had been part of the *Jaffree* litigation decided two years before by the Supreme Court, but Judge Hand bifurcated the claims challenging the silent prayer statutes after Douglas T. Smith, the parent of a pupil in the Mobile County schools, filed an intervening motion challenging the textbooks and other educational materials used in the county schools. Judge Hand concluded that secular humanism was indeed a religion because it rested on a foundation of ethical and moral beliefs designed to promote a world view, one whose "most important belief [was] its denial of the transcendent or supernatural." [94] He also ruled that textbooks that incorporated the views of secular humanism were prohibited from use in the public schools under the establishment clause because they had the effect of advancing one religion while inhibiting another.

The Eleventh Circuit unanimously repudiated Judge Hand's conclusion that the home economics, social studies and history textbooks in question violated the establishment clause on the grounds that they advanced religion. In rejecting the notion that the texts promoted the religious doctrine of "secular humanism", Judge Frank M. Johnson wrote that nothing about the "textbooks evidence an attitude antagonistic to theistic belief. The message conveyed by these textbooks is one of neutrality: the textbooks neither endorse theistic religion as a system of belief, nor discredit it,"[95] a result completely in accord with the establishment clause jurisprudence of the Supreme Court. *Smith* also marked the second time in less than five years that the Eleventh Circuit had overruled Judge Hand in a church-state case.[96]

If *Smith* remains notable in the annals of church-state law, it will be due to the eccentric pattern of constitutional interpretation that Judge Brevard Hand gave the First Amendment religion clauses. Challenging the use of home economics textbooks as an unconstitutional advancement of religion represents an imagination run amok; a more serious question for federal courts is the extent to which children should be required to use textbooks that parents maintain violate the sincere and fundamental religious beliefs of their children. If parents could make a genuine case, would school boards then have an obligation under the free exercise clause to accommodate the religious objections of the children? Could school boards accommodate their curricula to appease religious students without granting preference to one religion over another, a practice prohibited by the establishment clause? These genuinely serious and difficult questions presented themselves in another significant federal appellate case decided two years later.

In *Mozert v. Hawkins County Board of Education (1987)*,[97] a parents group calling itself Citizens Organized for Better Schools filed a lawsuit against the school board asking to withdraw certain portions of a textbook series published by Holt, Rinehart and Winston and adopted by the Tennesee State Textbook Committee for use in grades one through eight during the 1983-84 school year. Represented by Concerned Women for America, a conservative legal and educational foundation that consists primarily of evangelical and fundamentalist Christians, the parents claimed that some of the state-approved textbooks contained material that was antithetical to the beliefs of their children, including references to witchcraft, moral relativism and situation ethics, nontraditional sex roles, evolution, secular humanism and idol worship. Furthermore, the parents argued that forcing schoolchildren to participate in the Holt reading series over their religious objections imposed an unconstitutional burden under the free exercise clause.

In February 1984, Judge Thomas G. Hull of the U.S. District Court for the Eastern District of Tennessee dismissed eight of the nine complaints filed for lack of a constitutional issue. Three weeks later, Judge Hull granted summary judgment in favor of the school board on the remaining issue, which alleged that one of the challenged books taught that a person does not have to believe in Jesus to achieve salvation. Judge Hull found that although the "plaintiffs' religious beliefs were sincere and that certain passages in the Holt series might be offensive to them . . . because the books appeared neutral on the subject of religion, they did not violate the plaintiffs' constitutional rights."[98]

On appeal, the Sixth Circuit unanimously ruled that the lower court had erred in entering summary judgment because issues of material fact were raised which the school board had denied, including allegations that the plaintiff's use of the Holt series placed an undue burden on their religious beliefs. The Sixth Circuit instructed Judge Hull to decide "whether the defendants infringed on the plaintiffs' free exercise rights, whether a compelling state interest could justify such infringement and whether a less restrictive means could accommodate both plaintiffs and defendants without running afoul of the establishment clause."[99]

On remand, Judge Hull concluded that the students' free exercise rights were burdened because their "religious beliefs compel them to refrain from exposure to the Holt series," and that the school board had "effectively required that the student plaintiffs either read the offensive texts or give up their free public education." [100] The trial court acknowledged that the state had a compelling interest in ensuring compliance with education policies, but held that it could not "further its legitimate and overriding interest in public education by mandating the use of a single basic reading series," given that the objections of the students were rooted in sincere religious beliefs. [101] However, Judge Hull did not grant the plaintiff's request for an alternative reading series on the grounds that such an action would violate the establishment clause. Instead, he ruled that objecting students could excuse themselves from class and study independently, a practice the schools were obligated to follow.

On second appeal, the Sixth Circuit this time overruled Judge Hull on constitutional grounds, but issued three different opinions explaining its outcome. Judge David Lively, writing for the appellate panel, ruled that the district court had incorrectly relied on *Sherbert*, [102] *Thomas* [103] and *Hobbie* [104] in concluding that exposure to the Holt series placed an undue burden on the students' free exercise of religion. The Sixth Circuit distinguished the free exercise arguments successfully relied upon in that trilogy of cases to protect the rights of nontraditional observers with those at issue in *Mozert*. First, the court ruled that *Sherbert, Thomas* and *Hobbie* all involved "governmental compulsion to engage in conduct that violated the plaintiff's religious convictions." [105] In contrast, the requirement contested in *Mozert* that "students read the assigned materials and attend reading classes, in the absence of a showing that this participation entailed affirmation or denial of a religious belief, or performance or non-performance of a religious exercise of practice, [failed to] place an unconstitutional burden on the students' free exercise of religion." [106]

The Sixth Circuit also rejected the arguments of the plaintiffs that participation in the Holt series could be analogized to the requirement that the Jehovah's Witnesses salute the flag or face expulsion from school, [107] or that it was similar to the case in which the Amish parents argued successfully for their children's exemption from state school attendance laws. [108] In those cases, unlike in *Mozert*, the Sixth Circuit found there were "critical elements of compulsion to affirm or deny a religious belief or to engage or refrain from engaging in a practice forbidden or required in the exercise of a plaintiff's religion." [109] Concluding, the Sixth Circuit ruled that the free exercise clause did not afford students a constitutional right to refrain from participating in the Holt "critical reading" series because their exposure to some material might offend their religious beliefs. [110]

Judge Cornelia G. Kennedy wrote a concurring opinion agreeing that the students' free exercise claim lacked a constitutional implication, but added that even had she "conclude[d] that requiring the use of the Holt series or another similar series constituted a burden on appellees' free exercise rights," that burden would be "justified by a compelling state interest." [111] Furthermore, Judge Kennedy wrote that "if the opt-out remedy were implemented, teachers in all grades would have to either avoid the students discussing objectionable material contained in the Holt readers in non-reading classes or dismiss. . . students from class whenever such material is discussed," resulting in a "substantial disruption to the public schools" that Hawkins County had a compelling interest in avoiding. [112]

Judge Danny J. Boggs, the third member of the appellate panel, concurred that the school board was not constitutionally required to accommodate the students' religious objections to the Holt critical reading series, but disagreed with Judges

Lively and Kennedy that the basis for that conclusion rested upon the students' failure to implicate the free exercise clause. [113]

The federal courts have taken a more accommodationist tack on the discretion that public school officials have in allowing teachers and students to celebrate religious holidays during school hours. In *Florey v. Sioux Falls School District (1980)*, [114] the Eighth Circuit Court of Appeals rejected an establishment clause challenge to the policy of a Sioux Falls, South Dakota school district that permitted teachers and students to sing Christmas carols, perform religious plays and display religious symbols in the public schools. In affirming the decision of the district court, the Eighth Circuit found holiday observances to have a significance associated with the cultural and secular dimensions of American heritage, rather than the religious, and that such noted observances "no longer were confined or identified with the religious sphere of life." [115]

But *Florey* did much more than allow public schools to observe religious holidays. Technically binding on only that area of the country within the jurisdiction of the Eighth Circuit, *Florey* permits schools to sponsor the display of religious symbols in classrooms for instructional purposes and allows students to perform stage drama that celebrate matters of purely religious significance, assuming that in both cases the teachers conduct these observances in a "prudent and correct manner." [116] What is significant about *Florey* is that the Eighth Circuit limited its ruling to the facial challenge brought against the Sioux Falls guidelines. It acknowledged that the manner in which those guidelines are implemented could well constitute a violation of the establishment clause, but the resolution of that issue would have to wait until another day.

The Supreme Court declined to review *Florey*, which means that advocates of religious holiday observances can continue to rely on the Eighth Circuit opinion as authority. That does not mean, however, that *Florey* is law of the land and thus obligates public schools to permit religious celebrations. School officials do retain final discretion on whether to permit religious celebrations, with some jurisdictions opting for more restrictive guidelines than the Eighth Circuit ruled were constitutional. On the other hand, school districts across the country have adopted policies on religious holiday observances that are predicated for the most part on *Florey*. Still, the problem is far from settled, and school districts too often continue to celebrate, rather than to teach about, religious holidays in a manner insensitive to children of minority faiths.

Conclusion

Once considered a settled question of establishment clause law, the debate over government support for religious doctrine and practices in the public schools reemerged in full bloom in the 1980s. Legislative efforts to restore prayer in the public schools and to require that religious doctrine receive "equal treatment" in certain segments of the curriculum were struck down in the Supreme Court. Yet, religious accommodationists succeeded in those very same cases in forcing the Court to reevaluate the larger question of the proper relationship between religion and the public schools. The Court continued to repudiate legislation in which the state endorsed or participated in public school prayer sessions, but indicated that it might view differently statutes authorizing a moment-of-silence. Likewise, the Court rejected attempts to infuse religious doctrine into the public school curriculum;

however, it stated that under certain circumstances scientific theories of creation which differed from evolution may be presented in the public schools, including evidence disproving evolutionism.

But perhaps the foremost signal that the highwater era of a Supreme Court committed to keeping public schools free from state-endorsed religious preferences has passed came in the decision upholding equal access for student religious clubs in the public schools. The Court showed little or no appreciation for the genuine establishment clause problems that it acknowledged existed with the legislation, focusing instead on the rights of the students under the speech clause to conduct religious meetings on public school grounds, and concluding that their rights were equal to those of students at the college level. In one judicial stroke, the Court blurred the line it had long acknowledged existed between students at the secondary and college levels and left the door open for a more cooperative relationship between religion and the public schools on a number of fronts, including religious exercises, curriculum and, turning to the subject of our next chapter, government financial aid.

[1] 370 U.S. 421 (1962).

[2] 374 U.S. 203 (1963).

[3] Richard John Neuhaus, *The Naked Public Square* (1984).

[4] *E.g., County of Allegheny v. American Civil Liberties Union*, 492 U.S. 573, 109 S. Ct. 3086 (1989); *Bowen v. Kendrick*, 108 S. Ct. 2562 (1988); *United States v. Seeger*, 380 U.S. 163 (1965); *Torcaso v. Watkins*, 367 U.S. 488 (1961).

[5] For a more thorough discussion of the rise of conservative religious lobbies to political power in the early 1980s, *see* Hertzke, *Representing God in Washington*; and Reichley, *Religion in American Public Life* 311-38.

[6] 449 U.S. 39 (1980).

[7] Id. at 41-42.

[8] 472 U.S. 38 (1985).

[9] Id. at 40.

[10] Id.

[11] Id.

[12] Id. at 43 (emphasis added).

[13] *Jaffree v. James*, 554 F. Supp. 1130, 1132 (S.D. Ala. 1983).

[14] *Jaffree v. Wallace*, 705 F.2d 1526, 1535-36 (11th Cir. 1983).

[15] *Wallace v. Jaffree*, 472 U.S. 38, 60 (1985).

[16] Id. at 76.

[17] Four years later, the Supreme Court reaffirmed the constitutional ban on state-sponsored religious devotionals in the public schools when it declined to review *Jager v. Douglas County School District*, 862 F.2d 824 (11th Cir. 1989), *cert. denied*, 109 S. Ct. 2431 (1989). In *Jager*, the Eleventh Circuit Court of Appeals ruled that a Georgia high school's practice of recruiting Protestant ministers to give a religious invocation before football games violated the establishment clause.

[18] *May v. Cooperman*, 780 F. 2d 240 (3d Cir. 1985), *appeal dismissed, sub nom Karcher v. May*, 484 U.S. 72 (1987).

[19] 484 U.S. at 75.

[20] *May v. Cooperman*, 572 F. Supp. 1561, 1574 (D.N.J. 1983).

[21] Id.

[22] Id.

[23] *See Jaffree*, 472 U.S. at 62 (Justice Powell, concurring).

[24] The Equal Access Act of 1984, 98 Stat. 1302, 20 U.S.C. 4071-74.

[25] 454 U.S. 263 (1981).

[26] Id. at 265.

[27] Id.

[28] *Chess v. Widmar*, 635 F.2d 1310, 1317 (8th Cir. 1980).

[29] *Widmar v. Vincent*, 454 U.S. 263, 268 (1981).

[30] Id. at 274.

[31] Id.

[32] Id.

[33] 110 S. Ct. 2356 (1990).

[34] *E.g., Garnett v. Renton Area School District*, 865 F.2d 1121, *as modified*, 874 F.2d 608 (9th Cir. 1989); *Clark v. Dallas Independent School, decided without opinion*, 880 F.2d 411 (5th Cir. 1989); *Bell v. Little Axe Independent School District*, 766 F.2d 1391 (10th Cir. 1985); *Nartowicz v. Clayton County School District*, 736 F.2d 646 (11th Cir. 1984); *Lubbock Civil Liberties Union v. Lubbock Independent School District*, 669 F.2d 1038 (5th Cir. 1982), *cert. denied*, 459 U.S. 1159 (1983); and *Brandon v. Board of Education*, 635 F.2d 971 (2d Cir. 1980), *cert. denied*, 454 U.S. 1123 (1981).

[35] *E.g., Mergens v. Westside Community School Board*, 867 F.2d 1076 (8th Cir. 1989); *Clergy and Laity Concerned v. Chicago Board of Education*, 586 F. Supp. 1408 (N.D. Ill. 1984); *Bender v. Williamsport*, 741 F. 2d 538 (3d Cir.), *vacated and remanded*, 475 U.S. 534 (1984).

[36] 736 F.2d 646 (1984).

[37] 669 F.2d 1038 (1982).

[38] Id. at 1041.

[39] Id. at 1045.

[40] Id. at 1046.

[41] *Nartowicz*, 736 F.2d at 647.

[42] Id.

[43] Id. at 649-50.

[44] 766 F.2d 1391 (1985).

[45] Okla. Stat., Title 70, Section 11-101.1 (1981).

[46] *Little Axe*, 766 F.2d at 1399.

[47] Id. at 1397.

[48] Id. at 1411.

[49] Id. at 1407.

[50] Id. at 1407.

[51] 787 F.2d 1105 (7th Cir. 1986).

[52] *May v. Evansville-Vanderburgh School Corp.*, 615 F. Supp. 761 (S.D. Ill. 1985).

[53] Id. at 764.

[54] Id. at 766.

[55] Id.

[56] *May v. Evansville*, 787 F.2d 1105 (7th Cir. 1986).

[57] 865 F.2d 1121 (1989).

[58] *Garnett v. Renton Area School District*, 787 F. Supp. 1268 (W.D. Wash. 1987).

[59] *Garnett v. Renton Area School District*, 865 F.2d 1121, 1124-26 (9th Cir. 1989).

[60] Id. at 1126.

[61] Id. at 1127.

[62] 110 S. Ct. 2356, 2362 (1990).

[63] Id. at 2362-2363.

[64] *Mergens*, 867 F.2d 1076, 1078 (1989).

[65] Id. at 1078.

[66] Id.

[67] *Board of Educ. of Westside Community Schools v. Mergens*, 110 S. Ct. at 2370-2371.

[68] Id.

[69] Id. at 2373.

[70] 456 U.S. 263, 274 (1981).

[71] 110 S. Ct. 2356, 2369.

[72] Id. at 2393 (Justice Stevens, dissenting).

[73] Id. at 2393.

[74] Id. at 2384-85, 2391.

[75] Id. at 2391.

[76] Id.

[77] 393 U.S. 97, 99 (1968).

[78] Id. at 101-02.

[79] Id. at 98.

[80] Id. at 107-08.

[81] *West Virginia v. Barnette*, 319 U.S. 624 (1943); *Minersville School District v. Gobitis*, 310 U.S. 586 (1940).

[82] 482 U.S. 578 (1987).

[83] *Aguillard v. Edwards*, 765 F.2d 1251, 1257 (5th Cir. 1985).

[84] *Edwards v. Aguillard*, 482 U.S. 578, 591 (1987).

[85] Id. at 586-87.

[86] Id. at 603 (Justice Powell, concurring).

[87] Id. at 604.

[88] Id. at 627 (Justice Scalia, dissenting).

[89] Id. at 639-40.

[90] Id. at 628.

[91] 827 F.2d 684 (11th Cir. 1987).

[92] *Smith v. Board of School Commissioners of Mobile County*, 655 F. Supp. 939 (S.D. Ala.) *rev'd and remanded*, 827 F. 2d 684 (11th Cir. 1987).

93 655 F. Supp. at 980-81.

94 Id. at 980.

95 827 F. 2d 684, 692.

96 *Jaffree v. Wallace*, 554 F. Supp. 1104 (S.D. Ala. 1982), *rev'd*, 705 F.2d 1526 (11th Cir. 1983) (holding a series of Alabama school prayer statutes to violate the establishment clause).

97 582 F. Supp. 201 (E.D. Tenn. 1984), *rev'd and remanded*, 765 F.2d 75 (6th Cir. 1985), *as modified*, 647 F. Supp. 1194 (E.D. Tenn. 1986), *rev'd*, 827 F.2d 1058 (6th Cir. 1987).

98 *Mozert*, 647 F. Supp. 1194, citing 582 F. Supp. 201, 202.

99 *Mozert*, 765 F.2d at 79.

100 *Mozert*, 647 F. Supp. at 1200.

101 Id. at 1201.

102 *Sherbert v. Verner*, 374 U.S. 398 (1963) (holding that a state cannot prohibit unemployment compensation to individuals who refuse work based on religious convictions if those persons are otherwise eligible to receive them. In order to bar individuals who cite religious objections from receiving public welfare benefits, the government must demonstrate that such action (1) furthers a compelling state interest and (2) does so through the least restrictive means).

103 *Thomas v. Review Board of Indiana*, 450 U.S. 707 (1981) (ruling that the free exercise clause prohibits the denial of unemployment benefits to an individual who quits a job based on religious objections to the type of work required).

104 *Hobbie v. Unemployment Appeals Commission*, 480 U.S. 136 (1987) (holding that *Sherbert* standard applies to persons dismissed for religious objections to employment requirements, even if the religious claim was not asserted prior to beginning employment).

105 *Mozert*, 827 F.2d at 1065.

106 Id.

107 Id. at 1066, citing *West Virginia v. Barnette*.

108 Id. at 1067, citing *Wisconsin v. Yoder.*

109 Id. at 1066 ("In *Barnette* the unconstitutional burden consisted of compulsion either to do an act that violated the plaintiff's religious convictions or communicate an acceptance of a particular idea or affirm a belief. No similar compulsion exists in the present case."); id. at 1067 ("*Yoder* was decided in large part on the impossibility of reconciling the goals of public education with the religious requirement of the Amish that their children be prepared for life in a separated community. No such threat exists in the present case. . . .").

110 Id. at 1069.

111 Id. at 1070.

112 Id. at 1071-72.

113 Id. at 1074-75.

114 619 F.2d 1311 (8th Cir.), *cert. denied*, 449 U.S. 987 (1980).

115 Id. at 1316.

116 Id. at 1314.

CHAPTER THREE

GOVERNMENT AID TO RELIGION

After a period of relative quiet in the 1970s, a series of fresh challenges attacking settled establishment clause law governing the place of religious practices and doctrine in the public schools pushed the debate back to the center of the litigation stage during the 1980s. The coalition of religious and secular organizations possessing ties to the evangelical and fundamentalist right, most of which had climbed to positions of influence and power on the coattails of Ronald Reagan, also provided the financial, political and legal support for much of the litigation that asked the Court to reconsider its fundamental establishment clause jurisprudence that limited government support for religious practices and doctrine in the public schools. But President Reagan had also promised to press Congress and the state legislatures to provide more than just support for religion in the public schools. Also high on the conservative social agenda of the 1980s were efforts to increase the flow of tax dollars to religious schools and religious institutions. That debate, which had drawn the Court irrevocably into the thicket of church-state relations over forty years ago in *Everson v. Board of Education (1947)*,[1] had consumed much of the Court's establishment clause docket in the 1970s and continued to remain a central issue in the ensuing decade.

In a series of decisions that involved challenges to several state and federal parochaid statutes, the Burger Court had taken a firm line against direct and indirect aid to private, religious secondary and elementary schools for educational and support services,[2] with only minor exceptions.[3] However, the Court had developed less stringent rules for governmental aid to religious colleges, as long as the funds were used for nonsectarian purposes, such as building construction and remedial education services related to secular curriculum.[4] But for the most part, the parochaid decisions of the Burger Court had slammed the public coffers fairly well-shut on a wide variety of statutory schemes intended to benefit religious schools. For proponents of parochaid, how to restore the financial pipeline to government funds through more creative financing schemes became their principal cause of the 1980s.

Another component of church-state relations that continued to arouse division among the denominational representatives of organized American religion was the issue of tax exemption for religion. The Court had never given even the slightest signal that it planned to revisit its decision in *Walz v. Tax Commission (1971)*.[5] In *Walz*, an 8-1 Court, with only Justice William O. Douglas dissenting, held that tax exemptions for religious institutions did not violate the establishment clause because their purpose was to allow religion to flourish without entangling the government in its affairs. But the tax exemption cases that made their way to the Supreme Court during the 1980s encompassed more complex questions than those presented in *Walz*, reflecting the more sophisticated qualities that church-state litigation had assumed as a matter of general principle. In an observation that captures this dilemma well, one prominent legal scholar has commented that

> 'the wall of separation' metaphor may be a striking image, but, as with all jurisprudential formulas, care [must be taken] lest it serve as a substitute for reflection and reasoning. Even if we agree that the First Amendment was intended to erect a 'wall of separation between church and State,' that hardly tells us what it is that the wall separates."[6]

Indeed, as the foregoing discussion indicates, the Court itself continues to remain in considerable discord over the constitutional relationship mandated by the First Amendment religion clauses with respect to government aid to religious institutions.

Aid to Parochial Schools

Fashioning a set of constitutional principles that would provide a consistent approach to the problem of government aid to parochial schools was a responsibility that the Warren Court decided to leave to its successor. The one major parochaid case it decided, *Board of Education v. Allen (1968)*,[7] upholding a New York law that required the state to provide secular textbooks to students in religious schools without charge, came down at the close of the tumultuous era in which Earl Warren presided over the Supreme Court. In *Allen*, Justice Byron R. White, writing for a 6-3 majority, ruled that the distribution of secular textbooks to parochial school students did not violate the establishment clause because it possessed the "secular legislative purpose" of providing educational benefits to the student, not the religious school. To justify the New York textbook lending program, Justice White clearly relied upon the "child benefit theory" first articulated by Justice Hugo Black in *Everson*, in which the Court upheld a New Jersey statute authorizing the use of state-owned school buses to transport parochial students to and from school on the grounds that it extended "general State law benefits to all its citizens without regard to their religious belief."[8]

Ironically, Justice Black dissented in *Allen*, writing that "upholding a State's power to pay bus or streetcar fares for school children cannot provide support for the validity of a state law using tax-raised funds to buy school books for a religious school." [9] Justice Black, joined by Justices Fortas and Douglas, argued that the Court had misconstrued the child-benefit theory advanced in *Everson* to mean that governmental aid to sectarian schools was acceptable if legislative bodies could manipulate the language of their statutes to route financial benefits to the child, even though the actual recipient would be the school. [10] Armed with a substantial victory in *Allen*, parochaid supporters initiated much more intense efforts to pressure state legislatures and Congress to provide even greater funding for religious schools. [11] But three years later, the Burger Court took a major step back from *Allen*. In *Lemon v. Kurtzman*, the Court appeared to place a constitutional noose around all parochaid schemes when it announced a new, more comprehensive test to guide its establishment clause jurisprudence, a test that would have particularly bleak consequences for sectarian schools which sought funds from the public till.

In *Lemon v. Kurtzman (1971)*, [12] the Supreme Court struck down a pair of state statutes under the new tripartite test it developed to analyze establishment clause cases. Prior to *Lemon*, the Court had analyzed establishment clause cases under the *Schempp* standard, which required that statutes must have a secular purpose and neither advance nor inhibit religion. [13] Under the new standards announced in *Lemon*, the Court determined that a challenged statute or government action could only be held if it met three criteria: the statute must have a valid secular purpose, it must neither advance nor inhibit religion, and it must not foster government entanglement with religion. [14] Although the *Lemon* test has been subject to subsequent criticism from the Justices, [15] it remains, for now, at the operative center of the establishment clause jurisprudence of the Court. For the Pennsylvania and Rhode Island statutes reviewed in *Lemon*, the new standards proved fatal to the separate plans that provided direct governmental financial assistance to religious schools, including supplemental salaries to instructors who taught secular subjects, special educational services and textbooks. *Lemon* had the dual effect of turning off the governmental spigot which had enabled several states to funnel massive financial aid into religious schools while also putting into place more stringent judicial standards that parochaid programs were forced to meet in order to pass constitutional muster. From 1971 until 1985, the Court allowed only a few parochaid schemes to fall between the cracks of the *Lemon* test, striking down governmental aid to sectarian elementary and secondary schools in 11 of 14 cases that it decided with full opinions on this issue during this 14-year period. [16] Considering the chips that the Court had dug in Jefferson's metaphorical wall, its refusal to bring religious schools under the umbrella of governmental financial support at all levels must be viewed with welcome relief. But the decade began on a less than auspicious note.

Several parochaid decisions handed down in the 1970s had all but eliminated direct public assistance to sectarian schools, but the Court had shown greater leniency towards laws that granted indirect benefits to parents whose children attended religious schools if the parents of students attending public schools were eligible as well. The Court's first major parochaid decision of the 1980s, *Mueller v. Allen (1983)*, [17] involved a challenge to a carefully crafted Minnesota statute designed to relieve the financial burden of parents whose children attended religious schools. The statute authorized taxpayers who incurred educational expenses in sending their children to public *and* private schools to deduct from five to seven hundred dollars of those expenses from their taxable income. Tax-deductible expenses included tuition, textbooks and transportation. Although the Minnesota statute was facially neutral, it disproportionately benefited the parents of parochial school students, who were responsible for approximately 97% of the tax deductions claimed by parents after its enactment.[18]

Perhaps because it did not directly provide benefits to sectarian schools, but only to parents whose children attended them, a 5-4 Supreme Court majority upheld the Minnesota statute. Brushing aside the arguments made in the establishment clause attack on the statute, Justice Rehnquist, writing for the Court, held that the Minnesota tax-deduction program did not advance the sectarian mission of parochial schools because it applied equally across the board to all parents who had children in the state education system.[18] Justice Rehnquist also argued that the "effect" prong of the *Lemon* test posed no threat to the constitutionality of the statute, despite the fact, as Justice Marshall pointed out in his dissent, that the parents of the 815,000 students who were enrolled in state public education system did not, for the most part, receive tax benefits.[20] Finally, the Court reasoned that since the tax benefits were directed to parents, not to parochial schools, the statute did not violate the entanglement prong of *Lemon*.[21]

Mueller appeared to signal the beginning of a retreat by the Supreme Court from its post-*Lemon* decisions that had prohibited most forms of direct or indirect aid to parochial schools. But two years later, the Court confounded even its most hardened skeptics with its decisions in *Grand Rapids v. Ball (1985)*[22] and *Aguilar v. Felton (1985)*.[23] Together, *Grand Rapids* and *Aguilar* stand as two of the most important parochaid decisions of the Supreme Court to date for their explication of the limits on public assistance to parochial schools. Handed down on the last day of the 1984 Term, *Grand Rapids* and *Aguilar* reinforced previous Supreme Court precedent that barred government from providing direct or indirect financial aid to parochial schools for instruction in nonreligious subjects, teachers in parochial school classrooms regardless of educational purpose, subsidies for remedial education services that were otherwise available to children in public schools, or to help defray the cost of mandatory state testing and administrative requirements applicable to both private and public schools. While *Grand Rapids* and *Aguilar* involved separate challenges to state and federal funding schemes, the Court continued to hold on to its well-articulated principle that all forms of government financial assistance to religious schools, regardless of their legislative sources, which served to promote or advance religious objectives, or threatened to create excessive entanglement between government and religion, were unconstitutional.

Grand Rapids involved a challenge to two state-financed education programs offered to nonpublic elementary and secondary schools located in the Grand Rapids, Michigan, School District. Commonly referred to as the Shared Time and Community Education Programs, the school district offered substantive courses from its general curriculum to private school students on parochial school premises during regular and after-school hours. Teachers in both programs were paid by the school district. Alleging that the Michigan legislature had violated the First Amendment by authorizing funds to assist the educational needs of religious schools, a group of taxpayers filed suit in the U.S. District Court for the Western District of Michigan seeking declaratory judgment. In June 1982 the district court ruled that both programs were unconstitutional because they had the primary effect of advancing religion and because the administrative relationship between church and state resulted in excessive entanglement.[24] The Sixth Circuit Court of Appeals affirmed the lower court judgment on appeal.[25]

In July 1985, the Supreme Court, in a 7-2 decision written by Justice Brennan, held that the Shared Time and Community Education programs violated the "effect" and "entanglement" prongs of the *Lemon* test. In affirming the Sixth Circuit, Justice Brennan stated that the challenged programs had the impermissible effect of promoting religion in three ways. First, the teachers, paid by the state, were susceptible to the sectarian influence of the religious schools in which they were required to work, making it possible for teachers to advance religious doctrine at public expense. [26] Second, the symbolic union of church and state inherent in the programs threatened to convey a message of state support for religion to students and to the general public. [27] Third, the programs had the effect of subsidizing the religious functions of the parochial schools by taking over a substantial portion of their responsibility for teaching secular subjects. [28] Justice Brennan's opinion held that even the praiseworthy secular purpose of providing for the education of schoolchildren cannot validate government aid to parochial schools if the legislation has the primary effect of advancing one faith in particular or religion in general.

The program challenged in *Aguilar* was much narrower in scope than the one struck down in *Grand Rapids*. *Aguilar* centered on New York City's administration of a remedial education program falling under Title I of the federal Elementary and Secondary Education Act of 1965. [29] Under Title I, local educational agencies were eligible for compensatory education services and programs from the federal government if students under their jurisdiction were educationally deprived or from predominantly low-income areas. Federal regulations do not prescribe specific Title I programs, but instead encourage local school districts "to employ imaginative thinking and new approaches to meet the educational needs of poor children." [30] Federal law does provide, however, that parochial school students are eligible for Title I funds "on an equitable basis" if a local educational agency uses the funds for public school students. [31]

The Title I program administered by New York City consisted of instructional classes (remedial reading and mathematics, learning skills and English as a second language) and clinical services (guidance counseling and speech therapy). Each set of services was available to public and parochial students on their respective school premises. Title I regulations prohibit professionals who work in parochial schools from teaching religion or taking part in sectarian activities. New York City also required that all classrooms used for Title I services be free from religious symbols and references.

A taxpayer suit filed in 1978 in the U.S. District Court for the Eastern District of New York asserted that the administration of Title I funds by New York City educational agencies violated the establishment clause. [32] The complaint alleged the Title I program advanced religion because it resulted in a joint operating agreement between the government and religious schools. The taxpayers argued that the Title I program violated the nonentanglement requirement of *Lemon* because of the constant surveillance and monitoring which inevitably would take place to ensure compliance with its implementation guidelines. Nevertheless, in October 1980 the district court upheld the constitutionality of Title I and the New York City program. An appeal to the Supreme Court was dismissed for want of jurisdiction, [33] but both the program and the statute were again challenged a few years later. Based upon the record established in the earlier case, [34] the same district court granted summary judgment upholding the constitutionality of the funding program. However, in July 1984, Judge Henry J. Friendly of the Second Circuit Court of Appeals reversed the lower court, holding that supervision of the program had resulted in a relationship between the government and parochial schools that went far beyond the acceptable bounds of the establishment clause. [35]

The Supreme Court, although divided 5-4, affirmed the decision of the Second Circuit. Closely following the analysis of Judge Friendly, Justice Brennan, writing for the Court, held that the Title I program as administered by New York City violated the entanglement prong of *Lemon* on two accounts. First, the aid was provided in a pervasively sectarian environment. [36] The Court was singularly unimpressed by federal regulations requiring the removal of religious symbols from Title I classrooms. Second, because the federal assistance is provided through teachers, ongoing inspection was required to ensure their religious neutrality. [37] Justice Brennan further emphasized that the scope and duration of the Title I program would require a permanent and pervasive state presence in sectarian schools, noting that "agents of the State must visit and inspect the religious school regularly, alert for the subtle or overt presence of religious matter in Title I classes." [38] Justice Brennan concluded that the pervasive monitoring endemic to the New York City program struck precisely at the heart of the excessive entanglement problem the *Lemon* test was designed to prevent.

The fifth vote to affirm *Aguilar* came from Justice Powell, who wrote that the New York program raised entanglement problems conceptually identical to the one struck down in *Grand Rapids*. Chief Justice Burger and Justice O'Connor, who joined the opinion of the Court in *Grand Rapids*, dissented in *Aguilar*, with Justice O'Connor noting that "over almost two decades, New York's public schoolteachers have helped thousands of impoverished parochial schoolchildren to overcome educational disadvantages without once attempting to inculcate religion. Their praiseworthy efforts have not eroded and do not threaten the religious liberty assured by the Establishment Clause." [39] Justice Rehnquist was even more acerbic, accusing the Court of creating a "Catch 22 paradox. . .whereby aid must be supervised to ensure no entanglement but the supervision itself is held to cause an entanglement." [40] Though *Aguilar* drew sharp disagreements among the Justices, the separationist principles that emerged triumphant in *Grand Rapids* nonetheless survived intact.

Grand Rapids and *Aguilar* leave *Mueller* isolated among the Court's major parochaid decisions of the late 1970s and 1980s. Each decision had the important result of reassuring opponents of parochaid that the constitutional approach articulated in *Lemon* is still good law. Still, cautious optimism is warranted. The retirement of Justice Powell in 1987 and his replacement by Justice Kennedy, who has aligned himself with the Rehnquist-Scalia-White troika, dramatically weakened an already fragile separationist coalition. Justice Brennan's retirement in 1990 and his replacement by Justice David Souter may further compound this problematic state of affairs. This development has created a new opening for the Court's accommodationists to refashion its jurisprudence on the issue of government financial aid to parochial institutions, as two decisions in a related area since then have demonstrated is entirely possible.

Aid to Post-Secondary Schools and Other Religious Programs

Government programs that benefit religion at the post-secondary level of education or noneducational religious institutions have never drawn the same exacting scrutiny from the Court as legislation targeting elementary and secondary parochial schools. The Court has never developed a sophisticated constitutional analysis that justifies its two-tiered approach to government programs that aid religious institutions outside those boundaries. Its only offering has been an insupportable assertion that religion is a less coercive and politically divisive force in other, nonsecondary and elementary school environments, a view that rests on even more theoretically tenable grounds in light of *Westside v. Mergens (1990)*. Legislation encompassing broad issues of positive social welfare, such as government-sponsored programs to promote education for the handicapped and financial assistance to social service agencies for sex education and family planning counseling, draw sectarian institutions into the line of beneficiaries because of their traditional obligation to extend their hand in these areas. Those were precisely the issues at the center of two of the major government aid cases decided after 1985, *Witters v. Washington (1986)*[41] and *Bowen v. Kendrick (1988)*.[42]

In *Witters*, a unanimous Supreme Court held that a Washington state program that provided financial assistance to a visually handicapped student pursuing a postsecondary sectarian education did not violate the establishment clause. The Court ruled that funding provided by the Washington Department of Services for the Blind to Larry Witters, a 28-year old ministerial student with a degenerative eye disease, was intended to assist his individual educational progress, not the financial coffers of the sectarian college of his choice. In his opinion for the Court, Justice Marshall focused solely on whether the aid had the "effect of advancing religion," the second element of the *Lemon* test, and did not address its "purpose" and "entanglement" provisions.[43]

According to Justice Marshall, the aid could withstand an establishment clause attack on two fronts: First, the state program had a secular purpose—to assist the visually impaired in pursuing their educational and career goals; and, second, the aid to religion was indirect—state financial assistance was provided to the student and not to the religious institution. Taken together, the Court concluded that the Washington program "was in no way skewed towards religion. It does not tend to provide greater. . .benefits for recipients who apply their aid to religious education."[44] In the view of Justice Marshall, the effect of the statute was entirely benign.

Witters does not undermine the parochaid decisions of the Court that bar direct government financial assistance to elementary and secondary religious schools, but it does have a potential lasting effect on how the Court will approach future indirect aid cases at all educational levels. While not explicitly reaffirming *Mueller*, *Witters* does confirm that the Court has begun to take a less stringent view of indirect aid to religion if such aid is individual rather than institution-based. State legislatures looking to provide parochial schools with meaningful financial subsidies may increasingly take this route in future parochaid plans at the elementary and secondary school level. It could well be the first small step in a broader line of attack.

Two years later, the Court faced a very different issue involving government aid to religion in *Bowen v. Kendrick (1988)*. *Kendrick* centered on a facial challenge to the Adolescent Family Life Act (AFLA),[45] passed by Congress in 1981, which provided direct financial grants to public and nonprofit organizations, including those with religious affiliations, for adolescent sex education services. In addition to direct money grants authorized for religious institutions under the AFLA, its other key provision was that it prohibited funding to any institution that performed abortions, provided abortion counseling, or that advocated, promoted or encouraged abortion. On the basis of those two key church-state provisions, a coalition of taxpayers and religious leaders filed suit in the U. S. District Court for the District of Columbia challenging the law's facial constitutionality.

The lower court found no religious purpose inherent in the AFLA, but it did rule that the statute failed the second and third prongs of the *Lemon* test.[46] Religious institutions were the principal beneficiaries under the AFLA. Given the sectarian influence interwoven in the sex education provided by those institutions, it was impossible to conclude that the statute did not have the effect of advancing religion.[47] Moreover, the degree of government monitoring necessary to ensure that grantees having religious affiliations would not advance their religious doctrine in counseling and education services violated the *Lemon* nonentanglement requirement.[48] However, only a year later, the Supreme Court reversed and remanded the case for further review to determine whether grants dispensed and administered under the AFLA are implemented in a manner that violates the establishment clause.

Writing for a badly divided 5-4 Court, Chief Justice Rehnquist wrote that "it [was] clear from the face of the statute that the AFLA was motivated primarily, if not entirely, by a legitimate secular purpose—the elimination or reduction of social and economic problems caused by teenage sexuality, pregnancy and parenthood," and that benefits possibly accorded to sectarian institutions were "at most incidental and remote."[49] The Chief Justice also disagreed with the conclusion of the district court that the AFLA necessarily had the effect of advancing religion because the religiously affiliated AFLA grantees will be providing educational and counseling services to adolescents.

Moreover, the Chief Justice regarded as "unwarranted" a presumption that sectarian grantees were incapable of carrying out their functions under the AFLA in a lawful, secular manner.[50] Nor did he accept the conclusion of the district court that the AFLA is invalid because it authorizes "teaching by religious grant recipients on matters [that] are fundamental elements of religious doctrine, such as the harm of premarital sex and the reasons for choosing adoption over abortion."[51] Those, argued Chief Justice Rehnquist, "are not themselves specifically religious activities, and they are not converted into such activities by the fact that they are carried out by organizations with religious affiliations."[52]

Justice Blackmun, in a dissent joined by Justices Brennan, Marshall and Stevens, wrote "the record . . . is all too clear [that] federal tax dollars appropriated for AFLA purposes have been used, with Government approval, to support religious teaching."[53] The guiding intellectual principles behind the establishment clause jurisprudence of the Court were to prohibit government support for sectarian religious goals, regardless of whether those objectives advanced otherwise positive outcomes. Could the intent of the AFLA really have been, asked Justice Blackmun, to fund teaching that included the following:

> You want to know the church teachings on sexuality. . . . You are the church. You people sitting here are the body of Christ. The teachings of you and the things you value are, in fact, the values of the Catholic Church.[54]

Justice Blackmun also wondered whether the First Amendment permitted Congress to enact a measure that "encouraged the use of public funds for such instruction, by giving religious groups a central pedagogical and counseling role without imposing any restraints on the sectarian quality of the participation." He noted that AFLA funding would promote curricula that informed teenagers:

> The Church has always taught that the marriage act, or intercourse, seals the union of husband and wife, (and is a representation of their union on all levels.) Christ commits Himself to us when we come to ask for the sacrament of marriage. We ask Him to be active in our life. God is love. We ask Him to share His love in ours, and God procreates with us, He enters into our physical union with Him, and we begin new life. [55]

Furthermore, Justice Blackmun accused the majority of engaging in a constitutional sleight of hand in assuming that administrators of sectarian institutions would not

> breach statutory proscriptions and use government funds earmarked 'for secular purposes only,' to finance theological instruction or religious worship, in order to reject a challenge based on the risk of indoctrination inherent in 'educational services relating to family life and problems associated with adolescent premarital sexual relations,' or 'outreach services to families of adolescents to discourage sexual relations among unemancipated minors.' [56]

Justice Blackmun also argued that the AFLA, "unlike any statute this Court has upheld, pays for teachers and counselors, employed by and subject to the direction of religious authorities, to educate impressionable young minds on issues of religious moment," [57] creating "a symbolic and real partnership between the clergy and the fisc in addressing a problem with substantial religious overtones." [58] He concluded his displeasure with the majority opinion with an appeal to the district court that, on remand, it not "after all its labors thus far. . . grow weary prematurely and read into the Court's decision a suggestion that the AFLA has been constitutionally implemented by the Government," especially since it "eschew[ed] any review of the facts." [59]

In *Kendrick*, the Court indicated a new willingness to uphold government funding schemes explicitly intended to support the pedagogical goals of sectarian social-welfare services. Ignoring the "very real and important difference between running a soup kitchen or a hospital, and counseling pregnant teenagers on how to make the difficult decisions facing them," [60] the Court upheld, for the first time, a federal statute designed to subsidize religious teachings associated with an otherwise secular social program. Whether *Kendrick* amounts to a wholesale departure from the previous treatment that the Court had given to statutory schemes dispensing financial benefits to organized religion, or just an unwelcome aberration remains to be seen. For the moment, however, these and similar funding schemes have received the constitutional seal of approval from the Supreme Court.

Tax Exemptions

Considerably more enigmatic in the constitutional order is whether longstanding government policy exempting religious institutions from public taxation is consistent with the obligation of state neutrality towards religion required by the establishment clause. The Court has never felt compelled to reexamine its conclusion in *Walz v. Tax Commission (1970)*, in which it held that tax exemptions for religious institutions are not government subsidies assisting in the maintenance and establishment of religious institutions, but, rather, are indirect benefits available to non-profit secular organizations as well. [61]

As Chief Justice Burger noted in his opinion for the Court in *Walz*, "the purpose and primary effect. . .of tax exemption is not aimed at establishing, sponsoring or supporting religion. . .nor. . .is the end result—the effect—an excessive government entanglement with religion." [62] Few would dispute that the reasoning of *Walz* has its roots in tradition rather than constitutional mandate. The historical tradition of exempting religion from taxation, acknowledged Justice Brennan in his concurring opinion, was not "conclusive of its constitutionality. But such practice is a fact of considerable import in the interpretation of abstract constitutional language." [63] In developing this constitutional rule, the Court paid homage to the famous words of Chief Justice John Marshall that the "power to tax is the power to destroy," [64] and viewed tax exemption for religion as a positive means through which to maintain the integrity of church-state separation and religious freedom.

Nevertheless, tax exemption for religion is not absolute. Although federal and state law generally recognizes uniform exemption for the corporate structure of religion, legislatures and administrative agencies have enacted rules creating some important exceptions. Chief among those has been the power of the government, based on a showing of a compelling state interest, to penalize all tax-exempt organizations, including religion, which have engaged in conduct that is detrimental to a broader societal interest or conflicts with generally applicable criminal and civil laws. In the last decade, the Court has upheld the power of federal and state authorities to revoke tax exemptions for religious institutions under certain circumstances and to tax some profit-generating activities of religious entities. In a series of important decisions that elucidated the meaning of these new rules, the Court showed greater deference to government taxing power over organized religion. Perhaps no case illustrated the growing legal—and moral—complexities that exist in defining the power of government to tax religion than in the first and most controversial such case the Court confronted in the 1980s, *Bob Jones University v. United States (1983)*. [65]

Located in Greensville, South Carolina, Bob Jones University is a private, sectarian institution that places a special emphasis on the fundamental tenets of Christianity and the ethics revealed in the Holy Scriptures in its curriculum and code of student conduct. The university also believes the Scriptures teach that the races should live separately. As a result, Bob Jones refused to accept blacks for admission until 1971, when the Internal Revenue Service announced it intended to revoke the tax-exempt status of private schools that practiced racially discriminatory policies. In its view, such schools did not fall within the category of "charitable" institutions eligible for tax exemption under IRS regulations in order to further public policy. Bob Jones soon changed its admissions policies to allow blacks, but continued to compel the segregation of students on the basis of race as part of its regulations governing campus life. For example, university policy prohibited students from engaging in or even advocating interracial dating or socializing. Nor did the university allow racially mixed living arrangements for its students.

The IRS decided to strip the school of its tax exempt status later that year. Bob Jones then brought suit in federal district court to recover its tax exemption, claiming that its internal race relations policies were in accordance with sincerely held religious beliefs and therefore protected by the free exercise clause of the First Amendment.

The university prevailed at the lower court level, but lost when the Fourth Circuit Court of Appeals reversed, holding that Congress never intended for racial discrimination to find aid and comfort in federal tax policy.[66]

The Supreme Court agreed to review the case the following term, but soon after its decision President Reagan announced that the IRS had overstepped its authority in enforcing its new policy regarding racially discriminatory private schools. The Department of Justice then proceeded to file a brief with the Supreme Court in *support* of the position taken by Bob Jones University. Since that left the IRS without legal representation, the Supreme Court appointed William T. Coleman, a prominent Republican lawyer who had served as Secretary of Transportation under President Ford, to argue the case on behalf of the IRS. Not surprisingly, the position of the Reagan Administration drew widespread and passionate criticism from civil rights groups, which were astonished to find that President Reagan could lend the power and prestige of the federal government to behavior so wholly adverse to contemporary public policy as that of Bob Jones University. Ultimately, the Administration reversed its position and supported the IRS.[67]

In May 1983, the Supreme Court, in an 8-1 decision, held that the IRS had acted within its statutory authority when it revoked the tax exemption of Bob Jones University. Writing for the majority, Chief Justice Burger did not question the religious beliefs that underlay the discriminatory policies of the school, but concluded that the government has a "fundamental, overriding interest in eradicating racial discrimination in education...[which] substantially outweighs whatever burden denial of tax benefits places on [the school's free] exercise of religious beliefs."[68] Furthermore, Chief Justice Burger wrote that Bob Jones' educational mission was not consistent with public policy on issues of racial equity:

> Given the stress and anguish of the history of the efforts to escape from the shackles of the "separate but equal" doctrine of *Plessy v. Ferguson*, it cannot be said that educational institutions that, for whatever reasons, practice racial discrimination, are institutions exercising "beneficial and stabilizing influences in community life," or should be encouraged by having all taxpayers share in their support by way of special tax status.[69]

The Court had never held that *behavior* linked to religious *beliefs* is automatically outside the reach of government regulation prior to *Bob Jones*. Therefore, it is not surprising that the Court found tax exemptions to fall within the "belief-action" continuum that had long applied to other areas of religious free exercise. Having noted that the Court had never found all burdens on religious liberty unconstitutional, Chief Justice Burger asserted in *Bob Jones* that the government did indeed possess the authority to make an exception in its tax policy towards religion if the effect of those practices resulted in a "societal evil" not compatible with less restrictive means. Moreover, in striking down the tax exempt status of Bob Jones University, the Court sent a much needed signal to similar institutions that racial discrimination in the private spheres of conduct, no matter the pretense of its practice, would trigger government action to make that choice as costly and uncomfortable as possible. That, and not the sincerity of the religious-based objections to racial integration of Bob Jones University, was the larger meaning of its decision.

The Court also has ruled that less egregious practices stemming from religious beliefs are not exempt from taxation if the government can show that taxation serves an overriding governmental interest. In *United States v. Lee (1982)*[70] and *Bowen v. Roy (1986)*,[71] the Court refused to grant exemption from federal social security laws and regulations to the Amish and Native American Church on the grounds that certain government regulations are essential to ensure a reasonable degree of uniform compliance with federal tax regulations, even if the result is a burden on religious *practices*. In both cases, the Court affirmed the government's power to regulate religious practices on the showing of a compelling governmental interest, but acknowledged that it is virtually powerless to interfere with religious *beliefs*.

In *Lee*, the Court confronted the question of whether the free exercise clause shielded self-employed Amish from paying social security taxes. The Amish have a religious obligation to provide the same kind of assistance to one another that is provided by social security, rather than relying on governmental aid. The federal government argued that citizen compliance with federal tax regulations comprised a fundamental interest of the first order, and that any burden on religious beliefs would not threaten their integrity or observance. According to Chief Justice Burger, religious exemptions from generally applicable state laws were permissible but not mandated under the free exercise clause. In this instance, "because the broad public interest in maintaining a sound tax system is of such a high order, religious belief in conflict with the payment of taxes affords no basis for resisting the tax."[72] Writing for a unanimous Court, Chief Justice Burger ruled that no less restrictive or alternative means existed to accomplish "this most basic purpose of government."[73]

The Court faced a different question four years later in *Bowen v. Roy (1986)*, but pursued a similar line of analysis. In *Roy*, the Native American Church challenged a federal statute that required states to assign social security numbers to minors as a condition for their eligibility in the federal food stamp program. Two applicants to the program argued that a government requirement attaching a numerical identifier to their child would "rob the spirit from their daughter and prevent her from attaining power," a belief the Court did not deny was in accordance with the teachings of the Native American Church. The Court also acknowledged that Native Americans were constitutionally entitled to exemption from social security requirements under certain conditions.[74]

Here, the Court, in an 8-1 opinion written by Chief Justice Burger, held that "the Free Exercise Clause simply cannot be understood to require the government to conduct its own internal affairs in ways that comport with the religious beliefs of particular citizens."[75] Furthermore, he wrote,

> Just as the Government may not insist that [the Roys] engage in any form of religious observance, so they may not insist that the Government join in their chosen religious practices by refraining from using a number to identify their daughter.... The Free Exercise Clause affords an individual protection from certain forms of governmental compulsion; it does not afford an individual a right to dictate the conduct of the Government's internal procedures.[76]

The opinion of Chief Justice Burger demarcated a firm line between religious *practices* potentially detrimental to a broader societal interest—in this instance, maintaining compliance in the administration of federal welfare policy—and the power of government to interfere with sincerely held religious *beliefs*.

The constitutional questions raised in *Roy* and *Lee* were quite different than those at issue in *Bob Jones*, but the Court articulated similar analytical approaches in all three cases. First, the Court reiterated its long-standing view that religious practices, no matter how sincerely rooted in religious dogma, are not beyond the reach of government regulations. Second, the Court required the government to substantiate a compelling state interest that could not be accomplished through less restrictive means. Third, the Court continued to show deference to those legislative determinations reached by Congress on fundamental issues of public policy. It remained reluctant to grant legitimacy to religious practices or behavior that threatened to jar settled policy consensus.

The Court faced none of the fundamental issues that challenged state authority to regulate religious practices potentially adverse to the public interest, the common thread linking *Bob Jones, Roy* and *Lee*, in its two most recent tax exemption decisions, *Texas Monthly v. Bullock (1989)*[77] and *Swaggert v. Board of Equalization (1990)*.[78] In *Texas Monthly*, the Court was presented with a constitutional challenge to a Texas statute that exempted religious publications from state sales tax. *Texas Monthly* differed from the previous tax exemption cases in one elementary way: The publication challenged a statutory benefit already extended to religion, rather than requesting exemption from settled public policy.

Prior to 1984, Texas law exempted all magazine subscription income from state sales tax. In early 1984, the legislature amended the state tax code to repeal the general exemption and replaced it with a narrower provision exempting only those periodicals "wholly" religious in orientation. Texas Monthly, Inc., which publishes several news and business magazines, challenged the amended statute under the establishment clause, arguing that it accorded a benefit to publications that "promulgated the teachings of religious faiths" not available to secular publications, even those that discussed religion in an intellectual context. The plaintiff also argued that the amended statute violated the free speech clause because proper enforcement would require the government to examine the content of all published magazines to ensure that tax exemptions were accorded only to "wholly" religious periodicals. A Texas state district court agreed that the tax exemption violated the First Amendment, but the Texas Court of Appeals reversed.[79]

Reaching only the establishment clause question, the Supreme Court reversed, ruling 7-2 that the amended Texas tax exemption lacked a secular purpose because the benefits flowed exclusively to "wholly" religious affiliations. The Court long had upheld the power of legislatures to enact statutes that resulted in incidental benefits to religion as long as their primary purpose was to advance a secular interest. Since religious institutions were the sole beneficiaries of tax exemption under the Texas statute, the Court concluded that it was "difficult to view Texas' narrow exemption as anything but State sponsorship of religious belief."[80] The Court also rejected the defense that imposing the sales tax on "wholly" religious periodicals would unconstitutionally burden religious liberty, noting, as it had on numerous occasions prior to *Texas Monthly*, that public taxation of religion was not prohibited if it advanced a compelling governmental interest.[81]

In *Swaggert*, the Court unanimously agreed that California law requiring retailers and religious organizations to pay a sales tax on religious materials sold to the general public did not violate the free exercise clause. The issue arose when Jimmy Swaggert Ministries, a religious organization which conducts evangelical crusades, sponsors television ministries and engages in other missionary endeavors, challenged a California law that imposed a 6% state tax on commercial materials sold in-state and through out-of-state mail order, even though the materials sold by religious organizations furthered a religious objective. Writing for the Court, Justice O'Connor wrote that "the collection and payment of [a sales] tax imposes no constitutionally significant burden on appellant's religious practices under the Free Exercise Clause, which accordingly does not *require* the State to grant [religious organizations] a tax exemption." [82] The Court did not consider the establishment clause arguments raised by Swaggert Ministries. Justice O'Connor ruled that since California had not created a tax exemption solely for the sale of religious materials, which it ruled was unconstitutional in *Texas Monthly*, there was no basis upon which to reconsider the questions raised in that case.

Conclusion

Tax exemption provides government aid to religion, but its purpose, according to the Supreme Court, is to "permit religious exercise to exist without sponsorship and without interference." [83] The theoretical underpinning of tax exemption is found in the free exercise clause; it is to ensure that religion is not threatened by the taxing power of legislatures and to allow religion to flourish regardless of endowment. The Court has found that tax exemptions quite properly foster "benevolent neutrality" in the relationship between government and religion, a notion commanded in its view by the First Amendment's religion clauses.

But the Court has never held that tax exemptions are absolute, especially if practices emanating from religious beliefs result in egregious consequences for other individuals or significantly impair the orderly functioning of government. The Court affirmatively ruled in several cases that governmental bodies may impose tax burdens on religious conduct that conflicts with a more compelling governmental interest, whether that conduct involves the practice of race discrimination by religious schools, or failure to comply with generally applicable civil and criminal laws that do not unconstitutionally burden religious freedom.

Organized American religious denominations are in near universal accord on the constitutional status of tax exemption for religious institutions, but find themselves characterized by a greater cacophony of voices on the permissible level of indirect or direct governmental aid packages and subsidies to assist the sectarian goals of varied social welfare missions. The Court did not show the same willingness to retreat from its precedent on financial assistance to religious institutions as it did in its decisions granting religion a more symbolic and substantive doctrinal place in the public sphere. Yet, it did indicate that it would show greater deference to government aid to religion if the resultant benefits were indirect and not dispensed entirely to religious institutions. This view has been slow to evolve, but it is now enjoying a more widespread acceptance on the Court, which, having failed to articulate a consistent line of constitutional principles governing financial assistance to religion, has instead followed a pragmatic approach couched in policy considerations instead of constitutional commands.

[1] 330 U.S. 1 (1947).

[2] *E.g., Aguilar v. Felton*, 473 U.S. 402 (1985) (ruling the municipal administration of Title I of federal Elementary and Secondary Education Act of 1965 in New York City parochial schools violated the entanglement prong of the *Lemon* test); *Grand Rapids v. Ball*, 473 U.S. 373 (1985) (holding a state program that permitted public school teachers to offer general curriculum courses in parochial schools during regular and after-school hours violative of the establishment clause); *Meek v. Pittinger*, 421 U.S. 349 (1975) (striking down a Pennsylvania law allowing the state to furnish auxiliary support services to parochial schools); *PEARL v. Nyquist*, 413 U.S. 756 (1973) (ruling that a New York state funding scheme designed to relieve parents of parochial school students of tax and tuition burdens violated the establishment clause); *Lemon v. Kurtzman*, 403 U.S. 602 (1971) (declaring government grants and financial subsidies for parochial schools unconstitutional).

[3] *E.g., Mueller v. Allen*, 463 U.S. 388 (1983), *infra; Wolman v. Walter*, 433 U.S. 229 (1977) (upholding provisions of an Ohio statute permitting public school employees to provide in-house diagnostic services to religious schools and remedial services to parochial students off-campus, but striking down provision authorizing state reimbursement for educational services).

[4] *Tilton v. Richardson*, 403 U.S. 672 (1971).

[5] 397 U.S. 664 (1971).

[6] Bernard Schwartz, *The Ascent of Pragmatism: The Burger Court in Action* 188 (1990).

[7] 392 U.S. 236 (1968).

[8] *Everson*, 330 U.S. at 16.

[9] *Allen*, 392 U.S. at 252.

[10] Id. at 253-54.

[11] For a more comprehensive discussion of the politics of government aid to schools, *see* Diane Ravitch, *The Great School Wars* (1974).

[12] 403 U.S. 602 (1971), decided along with *Earley v. DiCenso* and *Robinson v. DiCenso.*

[13] *Schempp*, 374 U.S. at 205.

[14] *Lemon*, 403 U.S. at 612-13.

[15] *See* Chapter One, note 29.

[16] The Court struck down parochaid statutes in *Aguilar v. Felton*, 473 U.S. 402 (1985); *Grand Rapids v. Ball*, 473 U.S. 373 (1985); *New York v. Cathedral Academy*, 434 U.S. 125 (1977); *Wolman v. Walter*, 432 U.S. 229 (1977) (striking down, in part, provisions of an Ohio statute that permitted state reimbursement to parochial schools for special educational services); *Meek v. Pittinger*, 421 U.S. 349 (1975); *Wheeler v. Barrera*, 417 U.S. 402 (1974); *Sloan v. Lemon*, 413 U.S. 825 (1973); *PEARL v. Nyquist*, 413 U.S. 756 (1973); *Levitt v. PEARL*, 413 U.S. 472 (1973); *Norwood v. Hardison*, 413 U.S. 455 (1973) and *Lemon v. Kurtzman*, 403 U.S. 602 (1971).

The Court upheld parochaid plans in *Mueller v. Allen*, 463 U.S. 388 (1983); *PEARL v. Regan*, 444 U.S. 646 (1980); *Wolman*, (upholding section of Ohio parochaid scheme that allowed public school employees to provide diagnostic services and remedial services to religious schools); and *Lemon v. Kurtzman* II, 411 U.S. 192 (1973).

[17] 463 U.S. 388 (1983).

[18] Id. at 401.

[19] Id. at 397.

[20] Id. at 405 (Justice Marshall, dissenting).

[21] Id. at 402-3.

[22] 473 U.S. 373 (1985).

[23] 473 U.S. 402 (1985).

[24] *Americans United v. Grand Rapids School District*, 546 F. Supp. 1071 (W.D. Mich. 1982).

[25] *Grand Rapids v. Ball*, 718 F.2d 1389 (6th Cir. 1983).

[26] *Grand Rapids v. Ball*, 473 U.S. 373, 397 (1985).

[27] Id.

[28] Id.

[29] The Elementary and Secondary Education Act of 1965, 92 Stat. 2153, 20 U.S.C. 2740 *et. seq.*

[30] The Elementary and Secondary Education Act of 1985, 20 U.S.C. 2701.

[31] Id.

[32] *PEARL v. Harris*, 489 F. Supp. 1248 (S.D.N.Y. 1980).

[33] *PEARL v. Harris, appeal dismissed on jurisdictional grounds*, 449 U.S. 808 (1980).

[34] 489 F. Supp. 1248 (1980).

[35] *Felton v. Secretary, U.S. Department of Education*, 739 F.2d 48 (2d Cir. 1984).

[36] *Aguilar v. Felton*, 473 U.S. 402, 412 (1985).

[37] Id.

[38] Id. at 413.

[39] Id. at 431 (Justice O'Connor, dissenting).

[40] Id. at 420-21 (Justice Rehnquist, dissenting).

[41] 474 U.S. 481 (1986).

[42] 108 S. Ct. 2562 (1988).

[43] *Witters*, 474 U.S. at 485-87.

[44] Id. at 488.

[45] The Adolescent Family Life Act of 1981, 95 Stat. 578, 42 U.S.C. 300(z), *et. seq.*

[46] *Kendrick v. Bowen*, 657 F. Supp. 1547 (D.D.C. 1987).

[47] Id. at 1563.

[48] Id. at 1568.

[49] *Bowen v. Kendrick*, 108 S. Ct. 2562, 2571 (1988).

[50] Id. at 2575-76.

[51] Id. at 2576.

[52] Id.

[53] Id. at 2583 (Justice Blackmun, dissenting).

[54] Id.

[55] Id.

[56] Id. at 2589.

[57] Id.

[58] Id. at 2596.

[59] Id. at 2596-97.

[60] Id. at 2591.

[61] *Walz*, 397 U.S. at 674.

[62] Id.

[63] Id. at 681 (Justice Brennan, concurring).

[64] *McCulloch v. Maryland*, 17 U.S. 316 (1819).

[65] 461 U.S. 574 (1983).

[66] Id. at 582.

[67] For a critical discussion of the Reagan Adminstration's conduct in the *Bob Jones* case, *see* Lincoln Caplan, *The Tenth Justice* 51-64 (1987).

[68] *Bob Jones*, 461 U.S. at 604.

[69] Id. at 595.

[70] 455 U.S. 252 (1982).

[71] 476 U.S. 693 (1986).

[72] *Lee*, 455 U.S. at 260.

[73] Id. at 260-261.

[74] *Roy*, 476 U.S. at 696-97.

[75] Id. at 699.

[76] Id. at 699-700.

[77] 489 U.S. 1, 109 S. Ct. 890 (1989).

[78] 110 S. Ct. 688 (1990).

[79] *Bullock v. Texas Monthly*, 731 S.W.2d 160 (Ct. App. Tex. 1987).

[80] *Texas Monthly*, 109 S. Ct. at 900.

[81] Id. at 901.

[82] *Swaggert*, 110 S. Ct. at 697.

[83] *See Walz*, 397 U.S. at 674-75.

CHAPTER FOUR

RELIGION IN THE PUBLIC DOMAIN

For the better part of three decades after the landmark decision of the Supreme Court in *Everson v. Board of Education (1947)*,[1] the parameters of establishment clause law were set primarily through litigation that centered on state-sponsored religious practices in and government financial aid to the foremost symbolic microcosm of government—the public school system. Other forms of government support for religion in public life, such as the display of religious symbols on public property, government-funded legislative chaplaincies and celebrations of religious holidays, that raised possible establishment clause problems often were settled out of court through community relations efforts designed to avoid the political divisiveness frequently associated with church-state litigation. But in the last decade the resolution of these issues turned away from negotiation to litigation. The impact of those decisions wove major changes into the law of church and state, most of which appear destined for the long-term.

Religious Displays on Public Property

Perhaps no other area of church-state conflict generated as much controversy over such a short period of time in the last decade as did government-sponsored displays of religious symbols in public places. In communities across the nation, these practices were time-honored custom and tradition, as much as the lighting of Christmas trees or visits to Santa Claus at the local department store. Most of these holiday celebrations featuring religious displays are confined to the lawns of churches and synagogues and other private forums.

Thus, several of the controversies that materialized over the last decade, which seemed to increase exponentially with each passing year, centered on complaints brought by religious and civil libertarian organizations against the government-sponsored display of Nativity Scenes and other Christian symbols in public places during the Christmas season. Challenging public religious displays, especially during Christmas, had always been difficult for groups long active in this litigation, such as the American Civil Liberties Union, the Anti-Defamation League, the Baptist

Joint Committee on Public Affairs and the National Council of Churches, all of which share a deep and lasting commitment to religious tolerance. Public perception problems were even more acute to the separationist Jewish organizations. Their involvement was construed in some communities as an attempt to curtail the celebration of Christmas. Nevertheless, in the latter half of the decade with the support of the separationist Jewish civil rights and congregational groups, constitutional challenges were brought against public religious displays encouraged by segments of Orthodox Jewry that featured free-standing Chanukah Menorahs.

Unfortunately, litigation over public displays of religious symbols resulted in a confusing and often contradictory body of case law that clarifies little of the genuine establishment clause problems associated with this new legal genre of government preference for sectarian religion. Due to the badly flawed decisions issued by the Supreme Court in this area outlining the constitutional limits on public religious displays, the lower federal courts lack proper guidance on consistent juridical rules and thus remain in conflict over the permissible lines that can be drawn to sharpen the law. Having opened the door to this constitutional puzzle in the landmark *Lynch v. Donnelly (1984)*[2] and after exacerbating those problems in *Allegheny v. ACLU (1989)*,[3] two of its most fractured church-state decisions of the 1980s, the Court has created far-reaching implications for its future establishment clause jurisprudence.

In *Lynch*, the Supreme Court upheld the constitutionality of a life-size Nativity Scene owned and erected by the City of Pawtucket, Rhode Island, and displayed in a private park as part of that city's annual Christmas celebration. Writing for a badly split 5-4 Court, Chief Justice Warren Burger wrote that:

> notwithstanding the religious significance of the creche. . .when viewed in the proper context of the Christmas Holiday season, it is apparent that, on this record, there is insufficient evidence to establish that the inclusion of the creche is a purposeful or surreptitious effort to express some kind of subtle governmental advocacy of a particular religious message. . . . The creche in the display depicts the historical origins of this traditional event long recognized as a National Holiday.[4]

The Court overturned the decisions of the U.S. District Court for Rhode Island and First Circuit Court of Appeals, both of which held the Nativity Scene display to violate the establishment clause.[5] At the same time, Chief Justice Burger redefined the sacred qualities attached to the significance of the Creche in the Christian religions so that it would survive constitutional review. Government sponsorship of Nativity Scenes survived at the expense of the theological significance of this holiday symbol. A critical factor in the Chief Justice's Lynch analysis was the "secular context" in which the Nativity Scene was displayed. Because the Creche did not stand on its own, but alongside a facade of reindeer pulling the sleigh of Santa Claus, a Christmas tree and other secular ornaments, including multi-colored lights, candy canes and animals traditionally associated with the "winter holiday season," the religious significance of the Nativity became ancillary.

That the *Lynch* majority could find a government-sponsored display depicting the birth of Jesus Christ, whose life and teachings comprise the foundation upon which Christianity rests, to have a "legitimate secular purpose"[6] simply because it was placed next to candy canes and reindeer defies the imagination. Perhaps even more disturbing was the eager willingness of the Court to skirt so effortlessly through the traditional tripartite *Lemon* test to reach a predetermined outcome. The Court only half-heartedly applied the purpose-effect-entanglement test to the facts in *Lynch*, and instead opted for an "historical analysis" similar to the one it utilized in *Marsh v. Chambers (1983).* [7]

In a manner analogous to its treatment of legislative chaplaincies in *Marsh*, the Court found that the public display of religious symbols has been a well-established practice in the traditional American celebration of Christmas. Throughout his opinion, Chief Justice Burger likened the tolerance of public Nativity Scenes to other "official references to the value and invocation of Divine guidance" in American public life, including Thanksgiving, which was "celebrated as a religious holiday to give thanks for the bounties of Nature as gifts from God," [8] the "statutorily prescribed national motto "In God We Trust," [9] and the Pledge of Allegiance, which includes the phrase, "one nation under God." [10]

The Chief Justice wrote that it was clear that "Government has long recognized— indeed it has subsidized—holidays with religious significance." [11] According to the Chief Justice, these examples of government accommodation of religion are part of the American heritage and preclude a rigid, absolutist interpretation of the religion clauses that would result in reading religion out of public life. That, wrote the Chief Justice,

> has never been thought possible or desirable...nor required [because the Constitution] affirmatively mandates accommodation, not merely tolerance, of all religions, and forbids hostility towards any. Anything less would require the 'callous indifference' we have said was never intended by the Establishment Clause. Indeed, we have observed, such hostility would bring us into 'war with our national tradition as embodied in the First Amendment's guarantee of the free exercise of religion.' [12]

In a vigorous and forceful dissent, Justice Brennan, joined by Justices Blackmun, Marshall and Stevens, reacted to the conclusion of the majority with bewilderment for its casual dismissal of the religiosity of the Creche and its determination that legitimate secular goals—promoting commerce during the holiday season—were best served through municipal sponsorship of a religious display. Moreover, Justice Brennan found the syllogism posited by the majority, that the creche is a minor portion of a more inclusive public celebration of a national holiday, analytically bogus. Justice Brennan argued that the designation of Christmas as a public holiday did not mean that all forms of government association with it are constitutionally permitted. Furthermore, he argued that "plainly, the city and its leaders understood that the inclusion of the creche in its display would serve the wholly religious purpose of 'keeping Christ in Christmas.' " [13] He concluded, in even stronger language, with an eloquent and sensitive interpretation of the message sent by the Pawtucket display:

> [The Nativity Scene] is the chief symbol of the characteristically Christian belief that a divine Savior was brought into the world and that the purpose of this miraculous birth was to illuminate a path toward salvation and redemption. For Christians, that path is exclusive, precious and holy. [14]

But for those who do not share these beliefs, the symbolic reenactment of the birth of a divine being who has been miraculously incarnated as a man stands as a dramatic reminder of their differences with Christian faith. To be so excluded on religious grounds by one's elected government is an insult and an injury that, until today, could not be countenanced by the Establishment Clause. [15]

[T]he city's action should be recognized for what it is: a coercive, though perhaps small, step towards establishing the sectarian preferences of the majority at the expense of the minority, accomplished by placing public facilities and funds in support of the religious symbolism and theological tidings that the creche conveys. [16]

Despite the sweeping language of the majority opinion, *Lynch* did not put the issue of religious displays in public places to rest. Litigation following in the wake of *Lynch* and raising a number of new constitutional questions on several variations of government-endorsed public religious displays stemmed from the failure of the Court, whether through design or accident, to provide a definitive ruling. The results have been an even more puzzling series of outcomes that have further muddled the constitutional waters over the meaning and precedential value of *Lynch* and its progeny.

For example, the Court could have clarified the breadth of its holding in *Lynch* the following term in *Scarsdale v. McCreary (1985)*, [17] which involved the display of a privately owned Creche in a public park in Scarsdale, New York. Instead, the Court split 4-4 in its opinion, [18] thus letting stand the decision of the Second Circuit Court of Appeals, which upheld on free speech grounds Scarsdale's Nativity Scene display. Coming on the heels of *Lynch*, the Second Circuit based its decision on its finding that the public park in which the Creche was displayed qualified as a traditional public forum open to all types of expression—religious and nonreligious. This reasoning was crucial to the court's analysis:

[T]he Village's actions in permitting access to Boniface Circle for display of a creche—the same actions that would be necessary in permitting access for any display—do not lead it into such an intimate relationship with religious authority that it appears . . . to be sponsoring . . . that authority. [19]

Moreover, the Second Circuit rejected the argument that the Scarsdale Creche, standing alone on public property and devoid of secular trappings, could be distinguished from the *Lynch* display, which was augmented by less religiously obtrusive symbols. The court also found the Christmas celebration in Scarsdale did not differ significantly from the celebration described in *Lynch*. For years, the public park in which the Nativity Scene was displayed also had been host to government and privately-sponsored Christmas celebrations. In addition to the decoration of a Christmas tree and the singing of Christmas carols, the festivities had traditionally included a Nativity Scene.

Still, the Second Circuit concluded that the Village of Scarsdale did not intend to provide its imprimatur to the Christian faith at the expense of others, but to permit individuals or groups sponsoring religious celebrations to have the same access to a traditional public forum for the public expression of personal beliefs as nonreligious speakers. *McCreary*, which never carried precedential weight because of the tie vote by the Supreme Court, now lacks even symbolic importance because of further development of the law governing public religious displays. That irrelevance comes as a result of the most recent and even more analytically tortuous Supreme Court pronouncement in this area, *Allegheny v. American Civil Liberties Union*. [20]

Allegheny involved a consolidated challenge brought by the Greater Pittsburgh chapter of the American Civil Liberties Union against two religious displays sponsored by Allegheny County during the Christmas season of 1986-87. One consisted of an unadorned Nativity Scene displayed since 1981 by the Holy Name Society, a Roman Catholic group, inside the Allegheny County Courthouse and accompanied by a banner that proclaimed *"Gloria in Excelsis Deo"* ("Glory to God in the Highest"). The other was located one block down the street in front of the City-County Building jointly owned by the City of Pittsburgh and Allegheny County. In a novel factual twist, this display did not include a Nativity Scene, but a 45-foot Christmas tree and 18-foot Menorah standing side-by-side.

For several years, Pittsburgh had placed the Christmas tree outside the City-County building at its own expense and allowed city employees to decorate it with city-provided ornaments and lights. Beginning in 1982, the city expanded its holiday display to include the Menorah as a symbolic representation of Chanukah, the Jewish holiday that traditionally falls closest—but bears no relationship—to Christmas. The Menorah featured in the display was owned by Chabad, an Orthodox Jewish group formed by the Lubavitch, but it was stored, maintained and erected by Pittsburgh.

In December 1986, the ACLU filed suit against the county and the city, asking the District Court for the Western District of Pennsylvania permanently to enjoin both displays. Chabad was granted permission to intervene in order to defend the Menorah display. In May 1987, the district court issued an opinion refusing to enjoin either the Nativity Scene or the Menorah and Christmas tree, holding that each display was constitutional under *Lynch*. The district court stated that "the creche was but a part of the holiday decoration of the stairwell and a foreground for the high school choirs which entertained each day at noon." [21] Furthermore, the court concluded that the Menorah "was but an insignificant part of another holiday display," and that both "displays had a secular purpose" and "did not create an excessive entanglement of government with religion." [22]

On appeal, a divided Court of Appeals for the Third Circuit reversed, holding that the public displays of the Nativity Scene and Menorah impermissibly endorsed Christianity and Judaism. [23] The Third Circuit noted that each display "was located at or in a public building devoted to core functions of government." [24] Distinguishing the facts in *Allegheny* from those in *Lynch*, the court stated that, "further, while the Menorah was placed near a Christmas tree, neither the creche nor the Menorah can reasonably be deemed to have been subsumed by a larger display on nonreligious items." [25] The Third Circuit concluded that both the Nativity Scene and Menorah displays violated the establishment clause under the purpose prong of the *Lemon* test. [26] The Third Circuit refused to rehear the case *en banc*, but the Supreme Court granted *certiorari* and issued a closely divided opinion the following term.

Writing an opinion that resulted in each Justice, with the exception of Justice O'Connor, concurring in part and dissenting in part, Justice Blackmun upheld the ruling of the Third Circuit holding the Nativity Scene to violate the establishment clause, but reversed the lower court judgment striking down the joint Christmas tree-Menorah display. Justices Brennan, Marshall, O'Connor and Stevens joined the sections of Justice Blackmun's opinion striking down the Nativity Scene, with Chief Justice Rehnquist and Justices O'Connor, Scalia and Kennedy forming the majority to uphold the Menorah display.

Turning first to the Nativity Scene, Justice Blackmun wrote that,

> the creche in this lawsuit uses words, as well as the picture of the nativity scene, to make its religious meaning unmistakably clear. "Glory to God in the Highest!" says the angel in the creche—Glory to God because of the birth of Jesus. This praise to God in Christian terms is indisputably religious—indeed sectarian—just as it is when said in the Gospel or in a church service. [27]

Returning to the contextual analysis set forth in *Lynch*, the majority found that, in contrast to the Pawtucket case, nothing in the creche's setting detracted from the sectarian message sent by unadorned Nativity Scene. Justice Blackmun stated that, while "the government may acknowledge Christmas as a cultural phenomenon, it may not observe it as a Christian holy day by suggesting that people praise God for the birth of Jesus." [28]

But Justice Blackmun, in an analytical leap of faith, found no establishment clause barrier to the erection of the Christmas tree and Menorah in front of the City-County building. Retaining only Justice O'Connor from his ruling striking down the Nativity Scene, Justice Blackmun held that the combined display of the Christmas tree and Menorah did not have the effect of endorsing Christianity or Judaism, but simply recognized that both Christmas and Chanukah are part of the same "winter holiday season," which he maintained has attained a secular status in our society. [29] Placing the Christmas tree-Menorah display in the analytical framework established in *Lynch*, Justice Blackmun concluded that it could not be "interpreted as a simultaneous endorsement of Christian and Jewish faiths," but a conveyance of the "city's secular recognition of different traditions for celebrating the winter-holiday season." [30]

Rather than clarifying the issues raised in *Lynch*, the five opinions issued in *Allegheny* instead added to the considerable confusion that now surrounds this area of law. The section of Justice Blackmun's opinion striking down the Nativity Scene is an erudite and welcome endorsement of separationist establishment clause principles. The opinion prompted a blistering dissent from Justice Anthony Kennedy, which at times bordered on anger. Yet, one is at a loss to explain the difference between Justice Blackmun's Creche analysis and his interpretation of the Christmas tree-Menorah display as recognition of cultural diversity. [31]

This constitutional hair-splitting perplexed Justices Stevens and Brennan, both of whom dissented from the section of Justice Blackmun's opinion upholding the Menorah display. According to Justice Stevens,

> a lighted, 45-foot tree might convey holiday greetings linked too tenuously to Christianity to have constitutional moment. Juxtaposition of this tree with an 18-foot menorah does not make the latter secular, as Justice Blackmun contends. Rather, the presence of the Chanukah menorah, unquestionably a religious symbol, gives religious significance to the Christmas tree. [32]

Justice Brennan, in a separate opinion, was even more direct:

> The government-sponsored display of the menorah along side a Christmas tree also works a distortion of the Jewish religious calendar. . . . It is the proximity of Christmas that undoubtedly accounts for the city's decision to participate in the celebration of Chanukah, rather than the far more significant Jewish holidays of Rosh Hashanah and Yom Kippur. [33]

> Contrary to the impression the city and Justices Blackmun and O'Connor seem to create, with their emphasis on the 'winter-holiday season,' December is not the holiday season for Judaism. Thus, the city's erection alongside the Christmas tree of the symbol of a relatively minor Jewish religious holiday, far from conveying 'the city's secular recognition of different traditions for celebrating the winter-holiday season,' or 'a message of pluralism and freedom of belief,' has the effect of promoting a Christianized version of Judaism. . . . And those religions that have no holiday at all during the period between Thanksgiving and New Year's Day will not benefit, even in a second-class manner, from the city's once-a-year tribute to 'liberty' and 'freedom of belief.' This is not pluralism as I understand it. [34]

With *Allegheny*, the Court appears to have charted a jurisprudential course that effectively excludes any serious analytical treatment of the constitutionality of religious displays in public places. One tragic consequence of these cases has been the degrading treatment accorded to the theological qualities of religious rituals and symbols in order for religion to assume a contrived ecumenism sufficiently neutral to survive constitutional review under the establishment clause. Another has been to manufacture an artificial consolidation of divergent religious faiths under the rubric of a Judeo-Christian tradition embedded in American popular culture rather than recognizing the plural, multidenominational nature of American religious life, which encompasses much more than Judaism and Christianity.

Moreover, the narrow focus that the Court has accorded to the vibrancy of religious life in America has now been woven into its jurisprudence, the logic of which is increasingly escaping the Justices. This development was apparent in *Allegheny*, where much of the Justices' energy was devoted to accusing one another of not knowing what constitutes an establishment of religion. [35] Fratricidal relationships on a Court that is growing more intellectually galvanized than ever before in its church-state jurisprudence do not bode well for the future, especially if there is any hope for reconciliation of the Court's decisions governing religious displays in public forums.

Not surprisingly, a similar state of confusion exists in the lower federal courts as well. Cases involving almost identical fact patterns have resulted in disparate outcomes, often within the same federal circuit. For example, the Seventh Circuit Court of Appeals, which had affirmed a district court decision enjoining Chicago from displaying a Nativity Scene in the central lobby of City Hall in *American Jewish Congress v. City of Chicago (1987)*, [36] later reversed a decision from the Northern District of Illinois prohibiting the Village of Mundelein from maintaining a Nativity Scene on the lawn of the Village Hall.

In *Mather v. Village of Mundelein (1989)*, [37] the district court, distinguishing *Lynch v. Donnelly* and relying instead on *American Jewish Congress*, held the display violated the establishment clause and permanently enjoined the village from displaying the Creche. Two years after the district court ruling, the Seventh Circuit issued a *per curiam* order holding that *Lynch*, not *American Jewish Congress*, controlled *Mundelein*, and ruled that the Village was free to display the Nativity Scene during the Christmas season. Also noteworthy is the fact that the Seventh Circuit, which granted summary disposition, did not receive lawyers' briefs arguing the merits of the case. But the most startling aspect of this sequence of litigation is that the outcomes, reached after *Lynch* and decided in the same Circuit only two years apart, are nonetheless polar.

Mundelein directly contravenes not only *American Jewish Congress*, but the case upon which *American Jewish Congress* rests for authority. In 1986, the Sixth Circuit Court of Appeals ruled that a free-standing Nativity Scene displayed on the lawn of the Birmingham, Michigan, City Hall violated the establishment clause, distinguishing *Lynch* on its facts. In *American Civil Liberties Union v. City of Birmingham (1986)*, [38] the Sixth Circuit upheld a lower court ruling that neither *Lynch* nor *McCreary* controlled the facts presented in *City of Birmingham*. Unlike the Nativity Scene the Supreme Court found constitutional in *Lynch*, Judge Anna Diggs Taylor wrote that,

> [in this case the defendant asks the court to] discover an implied presumption in favor of the 'secularization' of the nativity scene, such that the religious symbolism apparent...should be somehow overshadowed, balanced or neutralized by the aura of Christmas shopping and holiday cheer. This court cannot so find.... The display conveys the restictive message that Christianity is the chosen religion of the City of Birmingham." [39]

In affirming, the Sixth Circuit agreed with the lower court that *Lynch* and *McCreary* failed to control the Birmingham Creche display, but corrected the rationale employed by the district court in finding it unconstitutional. The Sixth Circuit ruled that the Nativity Scene did not violate the purpose or entanglement prongs of the *Lemon* test, but did have the primary effect of advancing religion. Relying on *Lynch*, the Sixth Circuit found the Creche to have the "direct and immediate effect" of supporting Christianity because the city had failed to place identifiable secular symbols along side of it. [40]

The Sixth Circuit concluded that "it is difficult to believe that the city's practice of displaying an unadorned creche on the city hall lawn would not convey to a non-Christian a message that the city endorses Christianity, thus 'send[ing] a message to nonadherents that they are outsiders, not full members of the political community.' " [41]

The Sixth Circuit opinion was consistent with the line of decisions issued by other lower federal courts dealing with public religious displays before and after the *Lynch* decision. For example, shortly after *City of Birmingham* came down, the Seventh Circuit Court of Appeals, in *American Civil Liberties Union of Illinois v. City of St. Charles (1986)*, [42] upheld an injunction prohibiting the display of a cross on public property because it clearly symbolized the Easter holiday, even in a Christmas context. Likewise, in *American Civil Liberties Union v. Eckels (1984)*, [43] the Fifth Circuit Court of Appeals refused to hear the appeal of a decision issued by the U.S. District Court for the Southern District of Texas, which ruled that a display consisting of three Latin crosses and a Star of David, constructed and maintained in a public park, violated the establishment clause. In *Eckels*, the district court distinguished *Lynch*, ruling that the display of religious symbols by Harris County, Texas, failed the purpose and effect prongs of the *Lemon* test. [44] In his opinion, Judge Carl O. Bue, Jr., dismissed the claim of the county that removal of the religious symbols would result in the establishment of the non-theistic religion of secular humanism. Judge Bue wrote that the removal of the religious symbols did not result in hostility towards religion, but constitutional neutrality, and "safeguard[ed] the rights of minorities—in this case the rights of those who are not Christians and Jews." [45]

The deeply divided constitutional debate over the display of religious symbols on public land perhaps is best symbolized by the campaign launched by the Lubavitch movement in recent years to erect Menorahs in public parks and buildings. The focal argument offered by the Lubavitch is that the Menorah, according to the Talmudic definition of what constitutes a religious symbol, is not, in fact, religious. This argument has not found acceptance within the Conservative and Reform branches of Judaism, or among the national Jewish civil rights organizations. These disagreements have resulted in new litigation in which Jewish groups are reluctantly opposing each other in the courts. At the outset of the 1980s, Jewish civil rights groups and secular organizations took the lead in litigative efforts to prohibit the display of religious, primarily Christian symbols in public places; the decade ended with organizational representatives of the different branches of Judaism arguing in the federal courts not only the risks to church-state separation posed by government endorsement of public religious displays, but also the Talmudic and constitutional definition of the religious significance of the Menorah. [46]

The Lubavitch were unsuccessful in obtaining an affirmative injunction to display a Chanukah Menorah in *Lubavitch of Iowa, Inc. v. Walters (1986)*, [47] but the group attempted the following year to persuade the city councils of Tampa and Sarasota, Florida to permit the display of Menorahs on local public property. In each case, with the strong support and encouragement of local and national Jewish groups, the city denied the request of the Lubavitch movement. The Lubavitch organizations then brought suit, in separate actions, in U.S. District Court for the Middle District of Florida asking for injunctive relief to allow it to display Menorahs in Tampa and Sarasota.

After consolidating the two cases, *Chabad Lubavitch v. Sarasota (1988)* and *Chabad Lubavitch v. Tampa (1988)*, the district court refused to issue the requested injunctions, and ordered the parties to prepare for trial. But after failing to secure counsel, Chabad Lubavitch withdrew from the litigation, and the cases were dismissed in the fall of 1988, shortly before the beginning of the "holiday season." However, Lubavitch's failure to compel Tampa and Sarasota to display Chanukah Menorahs proved to be just a temporary setback. Less than a year later, the Supreme Court issued the *Allegheny* decision. Ironically, the Court rejected the contention of the Lubavitch movement that the Menorah lacked religious significance, and instead upheld its constitutionality based on the "secular" context in which it was presented. This will no doubt provide an incentive for the Lubavitch movement to continue its nationwide effort to display Menorahs in public places, despite the fact that it is the proximity of Chanukah to Christmas, not the lack of religious aura around the Menorah, that may account for the decisions of other municipalities to celebrate Chanukah in similar fashion. Most likely, opposition will continue to come from other segments of American Jewry, which continue to find themselves reluctantly drawn into a drama that is fast becoming a theatre of the absurd.

Religious Preferences in the Public Domain

Sponsorship of religious displays in public places is perhaps the most conspicuous example of government endorsement of religion, but it is not the sole problematic issue related to government preference for religion in the public realm. In separate cases earlier in the decade involving separate constitutional challenges to the power of churches to veto liquor licenses and to government-funded legislative chaplaincies, the Supreme Court faced significant questions on the relationship between government and religion, particularly the extent to which the state could show public preference for one religion at the expense of another. In another case that may reach the Court in the future, a federal appellate court confronted the issue of whether or not a state government could recognize Good Friday as an official, paid holiday. All three have implications for the permissible level of government endorsement of religion in the public domain.

In *Marsh v. Chambers (1983)*,[48] the Court ruled that the sixteen year-old practice of the Nebraska legislature of opening each day of its legislative session with prayer delivered by a state-employed chaplain did not violate the establishment clause of the First Amendment. For the entire sixteen-year period, which began in 1965, Nebraska had paid the same chaplain to provide invocational prayers before the commencement of legislative business. Prior to 1980, Chaplain Robert E. Palmer, a Presbyterian minister, began each morning with the following prayer:

> Father in heaven, the suffering and death of your son brought life to the whole world moving our hearts to praise your glory. The power of the cross reveals your concern for the world and the wonder of Christ crucified. The days of his life-giving death and glorious resurrection are approaching. This is the hour when he triumphed over Satan's pride; the time when we celebrate the great event of our redemption.[49]

Acting on a complaint brought by a Nebraska state legislator, Reverend Palmer removed all "explicitly sectarian" references to Christianity and began to open with a new, ecumenical prayer rooted firmly in the "Judeo-Christian" tradition. However, another Nebraska legislator, Ernest Chambers, filed a lawsuit in federal district court arguing that state-funded chaplaincies *per se* violated the establishment clause. The district court ruled that the use of public monies to compensate legislative chaplains violated the establishment clause, but it declined to enjoin the legislative invocations.[50] On appeal, the Eighth Circuit Court of Appeals held the Nebraska practice violated all three prongs of the *Lemon* test.[51]

Writing for a 6-3 majority, Chief Justice Burger held that "the practice of opening legislative sessions with prayer has become part of the fabric of our society. To invoke Divine guidance on a public body entrusted with making the laws is not, in these circumstances, an 'establishment of religion' or a step toward establishment; it is simply a tolerable acknowledgement of beliefs widely held among the people of this country."[52] The Chief Justice, finding no proof in the historical or legal record that the continuous service of the same legislative chaplain stemmed from an impermissible motive, did not find the Nebraska practice in conflict with the establishment clause.

Even more disturbing than the Court's reversal of the Eighth Circuit on the merits was its wholesale abandonment of the *Lemon* test in reaching its decision. The Court, after giving a cursory glance to the analytic framework employed by the Eighth Circuit, relied entirely on an "historical" analysis that celebrated the "traditional and time-honored" practice of beginning legislative sessions with prayer. According to Chief Justice Burger, the First Congress authorized the use of legislative chaplains through statute. "Clearly," he wrote, "the men who wrote the First Amendment Religion Clauses did not view paid legislative chaplains and opening prayers as a violation of that Amendment, for the practice of opening sessions with prayer has continued without interruption ever since that early session of Congress."[53] The Court provided no basis for its failure to scrutinize the Nebraska practice under the *Lemon* test, except perhaps for the unstated assumption that it could not have survived analysis under contemporary juridical standards.

The Court's aberrant departure from traditional establishment clause jurisprudence in *Marsh* remains befuddling considering that, during the same term, it used the *Lemon* test to strike down a Massachusetts statute authorizing a "church or school" to veto liquor licenses if the recipient establishment was located within 500 feet of either. Adding to the confusion was the fact that the 8-1 opinion in *Larkin v. Grendel's Den (1982)*[54] was written by an unusually forceful Chief Justice Burger. In affirming the decision of the First Circuit Court of Appeals, the Chief Justice wrote that "the statute enmeshes churches in the exercise of substantial governmental powers contrary to our consistent interpretation of the Establishment Clause by granting them veto power over public policy. Ordinary human experience and a long line of cases teach that few entanglements could be more offensive to the spirit of the Constitution."[55]

A more recent and perhaps more troubling case involving government preference for religion in the public milieu concerned a constitutional challenge to official government recognition of a religious holiday. In *Cammack v. Waihee (1987),*[56] a group of taxpayers brought suit against a Hawaii statute that designates Good Friday, the Christian holiday commemorating the crucifixion of Jesus Christ, as a state holiday. Unlike Christmas and Thanksgiving, which federal courts have found to have *de minimis* religious significance,[57] Good Friday bears no such place in the American tradition. The plaintiffs argued that the Hawaii statute represents governmental endorsement of a sectarian religious observance, a purpose incompatible with the establishment clause.

The U.S. District Court of Hawaii rejected the plaintiffs' arguments that the statute violated the establishment clause, both on its face and as applied, under the *Lemon* test. The trial court instead held that the Hawaii legislature, even assuming that it did "enact the Good Friday statute with sectarian purposes in mind, to allow the religious to worship on Good Friday and to allow the churches to call the faithful to prayer," intended to create a "needed day off from work" which could be used by its citizens to "emphasize those aspects of the holiday, the secular or the sectarian, which he or she chooses to emphasize."[58]

The Ninth Circuit Court of Appeals recently affirmed the district court in a split decision, ruling that "[t]here is nothing impermissible about considering for holiday status days on which many people choose to be absent from work for religious reasons."[59] The Ninth Circuit opinion relied heavily on the *Sunday Closing Cases*[60] and *Lynch v. Donnelly*[61] to reach its conclusion that establishing a state holiday to coincide with the Christian religious calendar accomplishes the constitutional goal of furthering a secular objective while, "at the same time, accommodat[ing] the widespread religious practices of its citizenry." [62] The court held that the Hawaii legislature furthered a valid secular purpose in creating a paid, state holiday on good Friday and stated, "nothing more is 'established'. . .than an extra day of rest for a weary public labor-force." [63] Noting that the Supreme Court, in *Lynch*, had interpreted the establishment clause to bar those practices having the purpose and effect of "endorsing" but not "accommodating" religion, the Ninth Circuit found that "[i]t is of no constitutional moment that Hawaii selected a day of traditional Christian worship, rather than a neutral date, for its spring holiday once it identified the need." [64]

As if this rationale did not already stretch even the outer limits of nonpreferentialist establishment clause jurisprudence, the Ninth Circuit also relied upon *Oregon v. Smith* to support government accommodation of majoritarian religion in an establishment clause challenge. The appellate court noted with approval the outcome in *Smith*, concluding that "the Supreme Court has recently identified as an 'unavoidable consequence of democratic government' the majority's political accommodation of its own religious practices and corresponding 'relative disadvantage [to] those religious practices that are not widely engaged in.' " [65] The Ninth Circuit's reasoning is baffling, since *Smith* did not involve government action taken on behalf of religion, but rather a challenge to a state statute that burdened individual religious rights.

Conclusion

Government endorsement of religion in the public sphere presents a quandary that goes directly to the heart of what the establishment clause was designed to prevent—government preference for religious values over nonreligious values and privileges accorded to one religion over others. The cases discussed in this chapter raise different moral and legal considerations than the establishment clause problems discussed earlier. One may argue that government endorsement of religion in public places, unlike government sponsorship of religious practices in the public schools, does not involve coerced conduct. Citizens are not *compelled* to view a religious display in front of City Hall; nor are most legislators in state legislatures required to acknowledge affirmatively a prayer prior to the opening of a session.

The case is fundamentally different for school children refusing to take part in "moments-of-silence" or to join student religious clubs. In those cases, the government, via its most potent and omnipresent symbol, the public schoolhouse, directly shapes the values transmitted to elementary and secondary school students. The potential isolation felt by students who do not subscribe to the majoritarian religious beliefs of a school district is real and constant for nine months of the year. Government financial aid to religious institutions is even more constitutionally problematic. Beyond the obvious establishment clause problems raised by the extraction of, to paraphrase Madison, "three pence" for support of the religious mission of sectarian institutions, government aid to religion requires dissidents to submit to the taxing authority of government without consent, posing a fundamental threat to the moral basis upon which representative government is based.

Still, government preference accorded to religion in the public sphere is, in many ways, even more offensive. Government-sponsored religious displays, although displayed seasonally, nonetheless put forth a clear message—that some religions are officially recognized and preferred above all others. Religious accommodationists argue that the solution is for the offended citizen to turn the other way; but that does not alleviate the pain, that does not reduce the isolation, and that does not eliminate the feeling by persons of different religious beliefs or no religious beliefs at all that they are merely tolerated guests in their own country.

Government support for Nativity Scenes and Menorahs signals to citizens identifying with neither that certain beliefs deserve official recognition, endorsement and celebration, and that others do not. So, too, does government support for legislative chaplaincies. The legislator whose religious views are neglected or offended through government-sponsored invocation can only step away. Legislative chaplaincies do not involve the same coercive measures that have doomed attempts at restoring religious exercises in the public schools, but the preferred status that sectarian religion is given in the civic culture communicates a disturbing message about the place of religious minorities and nonbelievers in American public life. Tragically, these arguments appear to fall on deaf ears at the Supreme Court, leaving separationists apprehensive about the future development of this component of church-state law.

[1] 330 U.S. 1 (1947).

[2] 465 U.S. 668 (1984).

[3] 109 S. Ct. 3086 (1989).

[4] *Lynch*, 465 U.S. at 680.

[5] *Donnelly v. Lynch*, 525 F. Supp. 1150 (D.R.I. 1981), *aff'd*, 691 F.2d 1029 (1st Cir. 1982).

[6] *Lynch*, 465 U.S. at 681.

[7] 463 U.S. 783 (1983).

[8] 465 U.S. at 675.

[9] Id. at 676.

[10] Id.

[11] Id.

[12] Id. at 673.

[13] Id. at 700-01 (Justice Brennan, dissenting).

[14] Id. at 708.

[15] Id. at 708-09.

[16] Id. at 725-26.

[17] 471 U.S. 83 (1985).

[18] Justice Powell, due to illness, did not hear the case and recused himself from voting.

[19] *McCreary v. Stone*, 739 F.2d 716 (2d Cir. 1984).

[20] *Allegheny*, 109 S. Ct. 3086 (1989).

[21] 109 S. Ct. at 3098, citing the district court opinion.

[22] Id.

[23] 842 F.2d 660 (3d Cir. 1988).

[24] Id. at 662.

[25] Id. at 661.

[26] Id. at 663.

[27] *Allegheny*, 109 S. Ct. at 3104.

[28] Id. at 3105.

[29] Id. at 3115.

[30] Id.

[31] Id. at 3138-39 (Justice Kennedy, concurring in part and dissenting in part).

[32] Id. at 3133 (Justice Stevens, concurring in part and dissenting in part).

[33] Id. at 3128.

[34] Id. at 3128-29 (Justice Brennan, concurring in part and dissenting in part).

[35] *See Allegheny*, 109 S. Ct. at 3106, 3110 ("Justice Kennedy's reading of *Marsh v. Chambers* [citations omitted] would gut the core of the Establishment Clause, as this Court understands it.... Although Justice Kennedy repeatedly accuses the Court of harboring a 'latent hostility' or 'callous indifference' towards religion, nothing could be said to be further from the truth, and the accusations could be said to be as offensive as they are absurd. Justice Kennedy apparently has misperceived a respect for religious pluralism, a respect commanded by the Constitution, as hostility or indifference to religion. No misperception could be more antithetical to the values embodied in the Establishment Clause."). *Cf.*, 109 S. Ct. at 3146 (Justice Kennedy, concurring in part and dissenting in part) ("The approach adopted by the majority contradicts important values embodied in the Clause. Obsessive, implacable resistance to all but the most carefully scripted and secularized forms of accommodation requires this Court to act as censor, issuing national decrees as to what is orthodox and what is not. What is orthodox, in this context, means what is secular; the only Christmas the State can acknowledge is one in which references to religion have been held to a minimum. The Court thus lends its assistance to an Orwellian rewriting of history as many understand it. I can conceive of no judicial function more antithetical to the First Amendment.").

[36] 827 F.2d 120 (7th Cir. 1987).

[37] 864 F.2d 1291 (7th Cir. 1989).

[38] 588 F. Supp. 1337 (E.D. Mich. 1984), *aff'd*, 791 F.2d 1561 (6th Cir. 1986).

[39] 588 F. Supp. at 1339-40.

[40] *ACLU v. City of Birmingham*, 791 F.2d 1561, 1564.

[41] Id. at 1566, quoting *Lynch*, 465 U.S. at 688 (Justice O'Connor, concurring).

[42] 794 F.2d 265 (7th Cir. 1986), *cert. denied*, 107 S. Ct. 458 (1987).

[43] 589 F. Supp. 222 (S.D. Tex. 1984).

[44] Id. at 234-35.

[45] Id. at 240.

[46] See the opinion of Justice Blackmun in *Allegheny*, 109 S. Ct. at 3094-97.

[47] 684 F. Supp. 610 (S.D. Iowa 1988), *aff'd*, 808 F.2d 656 (8th Cir. 1988).

[48] 463 U.S. 783 (1983).

[49] Id. at 823 (Justice Stevens, dissenting).

[50] *Chambers v. Marsh*, 504 F. Supp. 585 (D. Neb. 1980).

[51] *Chambers v. Marsh*, 675 F.2d 228 (8th Cir. 1982).

[52] *Marsh v. Chambers*, 463 U.S. 783, at 792.

[53] Id. at 788.

[54] 459 U.S. 116 (1982).

[55] Id. at 126-27.

[56] 673 F. Supp. 1524 (D. Hawaii 1987), *appeal pending*, No. 87- 15073 (9th Cir.).

[57] *See e.g., Lynch v. Donnelly*, 465 U.S. 668 (1984); *McGowan v. Maryland*, 366 U.S. 420 (1961).

[58] 673 F. Supp. at 1535-37.

[59] *Cammack v. Waihee*, 91 Daily Journal D.A.R. 4914, 4919 (9th Cir. May 1, 1991).

[60] *See* Chapter 5, note 78, *supra.*

[61] 465 U.S. 668 (1984).

[62] *Cammack*, 91 Daily Journal D.A.R. at 4919.

[63] Id. at 4922.

[64] Id. at 4919.

[65] Id., citing *Smith*, 110 S. Ct. 1595, 1606 (1990).

CHAPTER FIVE

THE FREE EXERCISE
OF RELIGIOUS BELIEFS

The religion clauses of the First Amendment ensure religious freedom through the twin guarantees of the establishment clause, which affirms the independence of religion from the state, and the free exercise clause, which prohibits the government from interfering with the right of individuals to hold, profess and practice their religious beliefs. In this chapter, our focus will shift from analysis of the establishment clause decisions of the last decade to litigation brought under the free exercise clause. Establishment clause litigation generally involves challenges to state action taken on behalf of one religion or to governmental preference for one religion over another. On the other hand, disputes arising under the free exercise clause usually result from clashes between individual conduct motivated by religious beliefs and secular law more attuned to maintenance of public order or safety than to accommodation of religious behavior.

The language of the free exercise clause is explicit in the prohibition it places on governmental authority to criminalize religious beliefs or to coerce individuals into accepting religious beliefs against their will. It is not, however, as crystalline in the protection it accords to religious *conduct* linked to those beliefs. As Supreme Court Justice Owen J. Roberts pointed out fifty years ago in the landmark case of *Cantwell v. Connecticut (1940)*,[1] "freedom of [religious] exercise" embraces both the freedom to believe and the freedom to act.[2] "The first is absolute, but, in the nature of things, the second cannot be. Conduct remains subject to regulation for the protection of society. The freedom to act must have appropriate definition to preserve the enforcement of that protection."[3] However, noted Justice Roberts, "in every case, the power to regulate must be so exercised as not, in attaining a permissible end, unduly to infringe the protected freedom."[4]

From 1940 through the early 1980s, the Supreme Court, following the direction charted in *Cantwell*, crafted a formidable body of case law that effectively placed most minority religious practices beyond the reach of government sanction. Central to its free exercise clause jurisprudence was the controlling principle that religious practices could not be unduly burdened absent a compelling governmental interest. The compelling interest standard carefully developed by the Court after *Cantwell* provided judicial protection for religious minorities whose beliefs, rituals and conduct would otherwise fall subject to the potentially harsh consequences of majoritarian rule.[5] Indeed, as Justice Robert H. Jackson eloquently wrote in *West Virginia v. Barnette (1943)*,[6]

> [t]he very purpose of the Bill of Rights was to withdraw certain subjects from the vicissitudes of political controversy, to place them beyond the reach of majorities and officials and to establish them as legal principles to be applied by the courts. One's right to life, liberty. . . freedom of worship and assembly, and other fundamental rights may not be submitted to vote; they depend on the outcome of no elections.[7]

The highwater mark for the protection of religious free exercise rights came in 1981 when the Supreme Court, in *Thomas v. Review Board of Indiana*,[8] articulated its most stringent constitutional burden required of the government in order to justify an infringement on religious practices. In *Thomas*, the Court upheld the right of a Jehovah's Witness to unemployment compensation after he was dismissed from his job for refusing to work on an armaments project that violated his religious beliefs. Chief Justice Warren Burger, in his opinion for the Court, held that

> the state may justify an inroad on religious liberty by showing that it is the least restrictive means of achieving some compelling interest. However, it is still true that 'the essence of all that has been said and written on the subject is that only those interests of the highest order, and those not otherwise served can overbalance legitimate claims to the free exercise of religion.'[9]

It appears now, however, that *Thomas* marked the beginning of the end of an expansive era in which the Court interpreted the free exercise clause to mean that most forms of religious conduct motivated by sincere religious beliefs were protected, even conduct otherwise prohibited by criminal statute.[10] After *Thomas*, the Court, for the remainder of the decade, departed dramatically from its settled line of free exercise jurisprudence in clear and convincing terms. The result may be a substantial erosion of the constitutional protection afforded to religious minorities. Furthermore, the Court not only became far less receptive to free exercise claims brought by religious minorities during the 1980s, but it also indicated that it was willing to reconsider the entire rationale upon which its free exercise jurisprudence had been built in the fifty years since *Cantwell*.

In *Employment Division of Oregon v. Smith (1990)*,[11] decided towards the end of the 1989 Term, the Court upheld an Oregon statute that criminalized the sacramental use of peyote, a hallucinogenic drug, by the Native American Church. More startling, the Court ruled that facially neutral statutes or regulations which burden religious conduct "need not be justified by a compelling governmental interest" standard of review.[12] In an opinion that could have far-reaching consequences for the degree of protection accorded minority religions in the future, the Court concluded that protection of religious practices is not presumptively the obligation of the courts, but preferably the political process. The Court reached this conclusion even while acknowledging that "it can be fairly said that leaving accommodation to the political process will place *at a relative disadvantage those religious practices that are not widely engaged in*," which the Court deemed merely "an unavoidable consequence of democratic government."[13] Government accommodation of conduct stemming from an individual's religious beliefs, no matter how central to the tenets of one's faith, does not appear to command more than deferential attention in the scheme of preferred constitutional values of the Rehnquist Court. The manner in which the Court arrived at its decision in *Smith* may be better understood through a review of its free exercise jurisprudence over the last decade, the subject to which the remainder of this chapter now turns.

Nontraditional Observers

Effectuation of the constitutional promise of religious freedom in the modern era came about largely through litigation brought by adherents of religious minorities whose unorthodox practices frequently encountered legislative proscription. Litigation brought by such diverse parties as the Jehovah's Witnesses, Seventh Day Adventists and the Amish, to name only a few, resulted in Supreme Court decisions that broadened the sphere of their religious freedom to unsurpassed dimensions. The constitutional protection accorded to their religious rights meant that the rights of other religious minorities flourished as well. Entering the 1980s, the status of nontraditional observers under the enlightened free exercise jurisprudence of the Court appeared to be quite promising. In a line of cases representing an amalgam of religious freedom claims, the Court had interpreted the provisions of the free exercise clause to include the practices of religious nonconformists as part of the diverse mosaic of American spiritual life. However, if the decisions of the Court and the lower federal courts over the last decade are indicative of a new direction in constitutional free exercise jurisprudence, then religious minorities have good reason to be nervous about their future status in the constitutional scheme.

The initial chill in the winds of constitutional change that blew through the free exercise jurisprudence of the Court in the 1980s came in *Goldman v. Weinberger (1986).*[14] Simcha Goldman, an Orthodox Jew, was a clinical psychologist and Captain in the United States Air Force when he was assigned to the March Air Force Base in Riverside, California in September 1977. Goldman, who also is an ordained rabbi, served as an Air Force chaplain between 1970 and 1972 prior to entering the Armed Forces Health Professions Scholarship Program to obtain his Ph.D in psychology. From 1977 to 1981, Goldman wore his yarmulke while on official duty without any reprisals from his superior officers. He had never been told that wearing a yarmulke while in uniform was problematic, and throughout his service he consistently received outstanding performance reviews and evaluations from his superiors.

In April 1981, Goldman, while testifying as a defense witness in a court-martial, was told, for the first time, that wearing his yarmulke while on duty violated an Air Force uniform dress regulation. The regulation, AFR 35-10, states, in relevant part, that "headgear will not be worn . . . [w]hile indoors except by armed security police in the performance of their duties."[15] Goldman was told by his superior officers to cease wearing his yarmulke while on duty. He refused to comply, and was then issued a formal letter of reprimand and threatened with court-martial proceedings. In addition, a positive recommendation that had been submitted on behalf of Goldman for a one-year extension of service in the Air Force was withdrawn and replaced with a negative evaluation.

Goldman, seeking to enjoin the enforcement of AFR 35-10, initiated a lawsuit in federal district court against the Secretary of Defense. He claimed that application of the regulation to prevent him from wearing his yarmulke unconstitutionally infringed upon his First Amendment right to free exercise. Granting the injunction, the U.S. District Court for the District of Columbia ruled that the Air Force had failed to show a sufficiently compelling interest that outweighed the free exercise rights of Goldman, and ordered the Air Force to withdraw the letter of reprimand and negative evaluation. [16]

On appeal, the D.C. Circuit Court of Appeals reversed, holding that the Air Force regulation was narrowly drawn and linked to legitimate military goals, which, in this case, meant the enforcement of a uniform standard of dress. [17] The appeals court acknowledged that the regulation was "arbitrary," but nonetheless ruled that the interest of the Air Force in uniformity and the traditional deference shown to the interests of the military did not require accommodation of what the court conceded was a legitimate First Amendment interest.

The Supreme Court, in a 5-4 decision notable for the very different conceptions of religious freedom beginning to emerge among the Justices, held that the traditional deference shown to the "professional judgment of the Air Force" in matters of military regulation included the enforcement of a uniform standard of military dress. [18] In affirming the appellate court, Justice Rehnquist admitted that "to the extent the regulations do not permit the wearing of religious apparel such as a yarmulke, a practice described by [Goldman] as silent devotion akin to prayer, military life may be more objectionable for [Goldman] and probably others," but nevertheless concluded that the military is under "no constitutional mandate to abandon their considered professional judgment." [19]

Concurring, Justice Stevens noted at the outset that "Captain Goldman presents an especially attractive case for an exception" from military dress regulations because of his sincere religious faith, the familiarity of a yarmulke and its symbolism, and because it serves as an "eloquent rebuke to the ugliness of anti-Semitism." [20] Furthermore, Justice Stevens wrote that a constitutionally required exception for Goldman would not disrupt the military, and even expressed distaste for the retributional tactics shown by the Air Force towards Goldman. Justice Stevens' greater concern, however, was directed to the consequences of creating a constitutional exception to AFR 35-10, envisioning future demands by Sikhs or Rastafarians for turbans and dreadlocks. He concluded that AFR 35-10 was written and enforced in a "neutral, completely objective" manner, and drew no distinctions based upon religious affiliation. An exception for yarmulkes would compromise the "true principle of uniformity that supports that rule." [21]

In his dissent, Justice Brennan noted at the outset that the Air Force had asked Goldman "to violate the tenets of his faith virtually every minute of every workday." [22] He also criticized the majority for failing to subject military regulations that burdened religious freedom to the same rigorous standard of judicial review traditionally applied to free exercise claims, and accused the minority of "abdicat[ing] its role as principal expositor of the Constitution and protector of individual liberties in favor of credulous deference to unsupported assertions of military necessity." [23] Moreover, Justice Brennan accused the majority of simply restating the assertions of the military "without offering any explanation how the exception Dr. Goldman requests reasonably could interfere with the Air Force's interests." [24] Had the Court "given actual consideration to Goldman's claim, it would have been compelled to decide in his favor."[25] Finally, in dismissing the arguments advanced to support the neutrality and objectivity of the regulation, Justice Brennan wrote that the practical effect of this distinction was "that under the guise of neutrality and even-handedness, majority religions are favored over distinctive minority faiths."[26]

In the aftermath of the *Goldman* decision, after considerable prodding by Congress, the U.S. Department of Defense adopted revised regulations permitting military personnel to wear "neat and conservative" articles of religious apparel as long as it does not interfere with the performance of military duties.[27]

A year later, the Court again deferred to the interests of governmental authorities to rationalize the suppression of free exercise rights when it decided *O'Lone v. Shabazz (1987)*.[28] Two Islamic inmates incarcerated in a New Jersey state prison requested an exemption from prison policies that burdened their ability to attend Jumu'ah, a weekly Muslim congregational service. Under the old security regulations, the Islamic prisoners were able to attend Jumu'ah services. But changes were instituted in April 1983 in prison policies governing the free movement of inmates throughout different sections of the prison. Ironically, it was those inmates subject to less stringent security classification who could no longer attend Jumu'ah services. After negotiations between the Islamic prisoners and prison officials failed to produce an agreement that would permit the inmates to attend religious services, the inmates filed suit in federal district court alleging that the prison policies constituted a violation of the free exercise clause. Upon review, the U.S. District Court for the District of New Jersey ruled that the prison policies regulating prisoner movement were reasonable and did not unconstitutionally infringe upon the free exercise rights of the prisoners.[29] The district court rejected the prisoners' arguments that the alternative arrangements were mandated under the free exercise clause, holding that the regulations on prisoner movement "plausibly advance[d]" the institutional goals of security, order and rehabilitation.[30] It concluded that the prison had enacted reasonable regulations related to legitimate phenological interests, and that it had adopted the least restrictive means available without "compromising a legitimate institutional objective."[31]

The Third Circuit Court of Appeals, hearing the case *en banc*, reversed the lower court judgment, ruling that the district court had not examined the prisoners' free exercise claim with the necessary judicial scrutiny.[32] The appellate court held that the prison shouldered a greater burden than the lower court's "reasonable" basis test when attempting to justify regulations that encroached on the religious rights of inmates. The Third Circuit concluded that the prison officials had not met the burden required by the free exercise clause of showing that it had attempted to accommodate the needs of the inmates through alternative means.[33] Writing for a 5-4 majority, Chief Justice Rehnquist reversed the Third Circuit, holding that the prison regulations, even though they had the effect of compromising the free exercise rights of the inmates, were linked to an important penological interest in a manner not inconsistent with the First Amendment. Furthermore, the Court ruled that the Third Circuit had erred in requiring the prison to show that more reasonable methods were available to accommodate the prisoners' religious conduct than the policies challenged. The Court's rejection of the Third Circuit's analysis continued the disturbing trend of deferring to "rationally-based" governmental objectives instead of using the compelling interest test established in *Sherbert v. Verner (1963)*, discussed in detail later in this chapter. Chief Justice Rehnquist wrote that "we take this opportunity to reaffirm our refusal, even where claims are made under the First

Amendment, to 'substitute our judgment on difficult matters of institutional administration,' for the determinations of those charged with the formidable task of running a prison."[34] The Court ruled that prisons, because of their special relationship to noncivilians, had no obligation to meet the compelling interest/least restrictive means test otherwise applicable in free exercise cases.

Dissenting, Justice Brennan argued that prisoners, even though they were no longer fully-enfranchised citizens, were entitled to have their constitutional claims, especially those alleging an abridgement of a fundamental freedom, reviewed according to the requirements of the *Sherbert* test. According to Justice Brennan, using the "reasonableness standard" endorsed by the majority as a jurisprudential vehicle to "review *all* constitutional challenges by inmates is inadequate to the task" of granting appropriate review to infringements of fundamental rights.[35] Lamenting the wide latitude that the Court granted the prison authorities in this case, Justice Brennan concluded that "[t]o deny the opportunity to affirm membership in a spiritual community. . .may extinguish an inmate's last source of hope and dignity and redemption. Such a denial requires more justification than mere assertion that any other course of action is infeasible."[36]

Doubts about whether the Court had, in *Goldman* and *Shabazz*, created exceptions for military and prison authorities to enforce policies not applicable to general civilian conduct or had grown less tolerant of religious behavior were answered the following term with its decision in *Lyng v. Northwest Indian Cemetery Protective Association (1988).*[37] The issue in *Lyng* centered on whether the free exercise clause prevented the United States Forest Service from building roads that would go through and around the Chimney Rock section of the Six Rivers National Forest, a national park historically used by Native American tribes for cultural and religious purposes. Studies commissioned by the Forest Service on the history of Native American cultural and religious sites in the area found that the entire Chimney Rock area was "significant as an integral and indispensable part of Indian religious conceptualization and practice."[38] The study concluded that building a road along any of the proposed routes "would cause serious and irreparable damage to the sacred areas which are an integral and necessary part of the belief systems and lifeway of Northwest California Indian peoples.[39]

The Forest Service rejected the report's recommendation that road construction cease. It selected another proposed route for the road that would have minimal impact on the identified burial grounds, but one which would still disturb the ritual and religious ceremonies of the Native American tribes. After exhausting all their administrative remedies, a coalition of Native American organizations sued the Forest Service in federal district court to enjoin the completion of construction on the proposed road. The U.S. District Court for the Northern District of California ruled in favor of the Northwest Indian Cemetery Protective Association and issued a permanent injunction that prohibited the Forest Service from building in the Chimney Rock section of the park or putting a timber-harvesting management plan into effect.[40] The Ninth Circuit Court of Appeals affirmed.[41]

Justice O'Connor, writing for a 5-3 majority,[42] reversed the judgment of the Ninth Circuit, holding that the government's action did not coerce the Native American tribes into violating their religious beliefs through compulsory action or threat.[43] Construing the free exercise clause in the narrowest possible terms, Justice O'Connor wrote that the government may not compel individuals to accept or act against their religious beliefs, but the clause does not prohibit state action that has an "incidental effect on certain religious practices."[44] Justice O'Connor did not dispute the devastating impact that the logging and road-construction projects would have on traditional Native American religious practices. Nonetheless, she concluded that the free exercise clause did not require the Court to "satisfy every citizen's religious needs and desires,"[45] especially when constitutional recognition of those needs and desires came into conflict with important and legitimate government objectives.

The pedantic approach of Justice O'Connor's *Lyng* opinion left proponents of broad free exercise rights considerably less sanguine over the future constitutional scope of permissible religious conduct. *Lyng* continued the troublesome pattern of constitutional reasoning that began in *Goldman* of showing far more deference to the stated objectives of governmental action which implicated the free exercise clause, even when the Court acknowledged that such action placed a substantial burden on religious freedom. Ironically, Justice O'Connor, in a sharply worded concurring opinion, criticized the similar, but more boldly stated, reasoning of the Court two terms later in *Oregon v. Smith*.[46] There, the Court shelved the compelling interest standard upon which it had relied in free exercise cases for almost thirty years in favor of a rational-basis test, a test for which she had helped lay the groundwork in *Lyng*.

Dissenting in *Lyng*, Justice Brennan, joined by Justices Blackmun and Marshall, argued that the Court had reached an "astonishing" conclusion. Continuing the line of criticism formulated in his *Goldman* and *Shabazz* dissents, Justice Brennan again chastised the Court for failing to employ a strict scrutiny analysis to actions of government "that frustrate or inhibit religious practice."[47] Justice Brennan also criticized the Court for the "noncoercive" test it used to analyze the free exercise claim at issue, arguing that the distinction it created between "governmental actions that compel affirmative conduct inconsistent with religious belief, and those governmental actions that prevent conduct consistent with religious belief" lacked merit.[48] Justice Brennan found no consolation in the semantics of Justice O'Connor, calling "such a distinction without constitutional significance."[49]

Justice Brennan also faulted Justice O'Connor for her "noncoercive" analysis in *Lyng*, arguing that "[Native Americans] will not derive any solace from the knowledge that although the practice of their religion will become more difficult as a result of the [g]overnment's actions, they are free to maintain their religious beliefs."[50] The "noncoercive" test that Justice O'Connor formulated in *Lyng* distinguished between the permissible regulation of religious belief and that of conduct linked to religious beliefs, a distinction that Justice Scalia followed to the letter in *Smith*.[51] Justice O'Connor acknowledged in *Lyng* that government still carried the burden of showing that, in free exercise cases, the challenged regulations must advance a compelling interest. The result reached in *Lyng*, though, with its attendant lack of concern to the consequences of state action, provided the analytical foundation for the outcome in *Smith*. Despite her protests in *Smith*, Justice O'Connor influenced the logical development of the free exercise jurisprudence of the Court to no small degree.

Two of the more significant free exercise cases decided in the lower federal courts during the 1980s, *Menora v. Illinois High School Association (1982)*[52] and *Paul v. Watchtower Bible and Tract Society (1987)*,[53] provide illuminating examples of the dual standards of review applicable to belief and conduct.

Menora concerned a challenge to an Illinois High School Association (IHSA) regulation that forbade high school basketball players taking part in interscholastic competition from wearing headwear, other than a two-inch headband, while on the court. Moshe Menora and several other Jewish basketball players filed suit in federal district court against the ISHA, arguing that the regulation amounted to a violation of the free exercise clause of the First Amendment because it had the effect of prohibiting Orthodox Jews from wearing their yarmulkes during games. Citing the severe burden imposed on the ability of the basketball players to fulfill their religious obligations, Judge Milton I. Shadur of the U.S. District Court for the Northern District of Illinois struck down the regulation as violative of the free exercise clause. The court concluded that the potential safety hazards posed by allowing Orthodox Jews to wear their yarmulkes during competition were too slight to warrant placing before the students the dilemma of choosing between their religious observance and participating in interscholastic basketball. [54]

The IHSA appealed the judgment, arguing that the regulation did not implicate the free exercise clause and that its sole purpose was to ensure the safety of individuals engaged in organized competition under its supervision. A divided Seventh Circuit Court of Appeals agreed with the IHSA, ruling that the regulation against headgear during competition did not infringe the free exercise rights of Orthodox Jewish basketball players. Judge Richard Posner, who would dissent five years later from the Seventh Circuit decision in *American Jewish Congress v. Chicago (1987)* striking down a state-sponsored Nativity Scene, [55] held that the IHSA had not placed the Jewish basketball players in the position of sacrificing their religion for citizenship, but that it had only forced "orthodox Jews to choose. . . between keeping their heads covered and playing interscholastic basketball." [56]

However, Judge Posner did not order the lower court to dismiss its earlier ruling. Instead, he ordered the decision vacated and remanded for further proceedings to allow the Orthodox Jewish students "an opportunity to propose to the Association a form of secure head covering that complies with Jewish law yet meets the Association's safety concerns." [57] Still, the Seventh Circuit indicated greater concern for the interests of the IHSA than it did for the consequences of the regulation, which it dismissed as having a *de minimis* impact on Orthodox Jewish athletes. [58] Indeed, Judge Posner concluded that the regulation constituted nothing more than a "nonexistent burden on religious observance." [59]

The facts presented in *Paul v. Watchtower Bible and Tract Society* introduced a much more novel issue to the free exercise debate than the traditional recurring themes of whether the government or private employers are constitutionally required to accommodate certain forms of religiously-motivated conduct. [60] Instead, *Paul* involved the question of whether the free exercise clause protects individuals from tort liability when the alleged injuries associated with tortious conduct are motivated by religious beliefs.

Janice Paul was raised in a family of devout Jehovah's Witnesses. From her baptism at age 16, when she became an official member of the church, until she voluntarily left the Witnesses at 24, Paul attended church an average of 20 hours per month, and spent an estimated 40 hours per week proselytizing and distributing Witnesses' publications door-to-door. She also married another member of the Jehovah's Witnesses.

In 1975, Paul's parents were "disfellowshipped" from the Jehovah's Witnesses. In the rules governing membership in the Witnesses, disfellowshipped persons are former members who were excommunicated from the church. Members of the Witnesses are prohibited from acknowledging or engaging in any communication with these former members. This practice is known in the Witnesses' community as "shunning." Shunning is derived from a similar practice associated with early Christianity. Other religious groups in the United States, including the Amish and Mennonites, also practice a form of shunning.

Although Paul was still a member of the Witnesses when her parents were disfellowshipped in early 1975, she was permitted, under church rules, to communicate with them about family matters, but not on any other subject. In November 1975, a few months after her parents were excommunicated, Paul, having decided that her parents had been unfairly disfellowshipped, left the Witnesses. Until 1981, members who left the Witnesses on their own volition were not subject to shunning from other members. In fact, when Paul left the Witnesses, she was not subject to any sanction, and continued to associate with her friends on secular subjects who were still members of the church. Under church rules she became a "disassociated" person.

In September 1981, the Governing Body of Jehovah's Witnesses issued a new interpretation of rules regarding member relationships with disassociated persons. The distinction between disfellowshipped and disassociated individuals was abolished, and, from then on, all former members were to be shunned. Paul consequently found herself ostracized from friends and church members whom she had known for almost her entire life. Upset by her shunning, Paul initiated a civil suit against the Watchtower and Bible Tract Society, claiming that the shunning she was subjected to resulted in defamation, fraud, invasion of privacy and outrageous conduct, all of which entitled her to damages under tort law. Watchtower moved for summary dismissal of the case, arguing that shunning is religious conduct protected by the free exercise provisions of both the Washington and United States Constitutions.

The U.S. District Court for the Western District of Washington denied the Witnesses' motion to dismiss the suit, but it did, in the alternative, grant summary judgment on their behalf. The district court held that shunning among members of religious faiths was an ecclesiastical, not civil, practice. Courts were thus prohibited from determining issues of canon law based on the ecclesiastical abstention doctrine. Moreover, the court held that the Witnesses' practice of shunning was protected under state and federal constitutional law. [61]

The Ninth Circuit Court of Appeals unanimously affirmed the lower court, holding that the "members of the Church Paul decided to abandon have concluded that they no longer want to associate with her. . . [and] they are free to make that choice. The Jehovah's Witnesses practice of shunning is protected under the First Amendment of the United States Constitution and therefore under the provisions of the Washington state constitution." [62] The Ninth Circuit also held that the Witnesses' defense to Janice Paul's cause of action amounted to a "defense of privilege." [63] It concluded that "permitting [Paul] to recover for intangible or emotional injuries would unconstitutionally restrict the Jehovah's Witnesses free exercise of religion. . . and that the constitutional guarantee of the free exercise of religion requires that society tolerate the type of harms suffered by Paul as a price well-worth paying to safeguard the right of religious difference[s] that all citizens enjoy." [64]

Religious Conduct in the Public Forum

Proselytization, or the personal efforts to convert other individuals from one religion to another, is central to the evangelical mission of numerous faith communities in the United States. Religions that embrace personal evangelism as part of their larger institutional mission to spread their beliefs comprise a minority of the American religious population. Several of the more well-known religions that consider the public forum an arena for proselytization, including the Jehovah's Witnesses, Hari Krishnas and Scientologists, meet public resistance and even antipathy for what is viewed as unorthodox conduct. Disfavored religions historically have faced popular resistance in their quest for equal protection under the law, especially protection sought for religious practices conducted in public places.

Religious persecution through legislation in the United States is most commonly, although certainly not exclusively, associated with efforts directed against the Jehovah's Witnesses. Indeed, the Witnesses, through a largely successful litigation campaign that began in the late 1930s and has continued virtually uninterrupted to this day, are almost singularly responsible for the modern understanding of the free exercise clause as it applies to religious activities in public places. Litigation brought by the Witnesses attacking state and local laws that prohibited proselytizing and other forms of religious conduct in public places including parks, sidewalks and street corners, has been continuous and immensely successful, securing constitutional protection for the rights of all faiths. [65]

Nonetheless, constitutional development in this area has stopped short of guaranteeing religious groups absolute access to the public forum. The federal courts, though drawing appropriate time, place and manner regulations, have placed disputes over access to the public forum for religious purposes within a similar, though not identical, analytical framework as cases involving access for nonreligious, or political, speech. The Supreme Court handed down two cases resting on free speech principles during the 1980s that illustrate the constitutional boundaries of permissible religious conduct in public places.

In *Heffron v. International Society for Krishna Consciousness (ISKCON) (1981),* [66] the Court upheld a Minnesota state law that prohibited individuals and groups from distributing or selling merchandise, or soliciting funds at the state fair, except at "duly authorized" locations. The statute did not forbid individuals and groups from communicating with others while walking around the fairgrounds, but it did relegate all sales, distribution and solicitation of funds to designated booths. The Hari Krishnas brought suit in state district court to have the rule enjoined on constitutional grounds, arguing that it violated the free speech and free exercise clauses of the First Amendment. Enforcement of the statute, charged the Krishnas, suppressed their ability to engage in Sankirtan, a religious ritual that requires the Krishnas to distribute religious literature and solicit contributions in public places. The Krishnas also argued that the law prohibited the free movement which is so central to Sankirtan. The district court rejected the Krishna's arguments. On appeal, the Minnesota Supreme Court affirmed. [67]

The U.S. Supreme Court, in an opinion written by Justice Byron White, held that the Minnesota statute was a permissible content-neutral restriction narrowly drawn to achieve the compelling governmental interest of crowd control at a large public gathering. Justice White, acknowledging that Sankirtan constituted communicative conduct, ruled that the primary purpose of the statute was not to suppress the right of the Krishnas to proselytize or impair their ability to communicate, but to establish reasonable time, place and manner regulations applicable to all individuals and groups. [68] Moreover, alternative forums were available to the Krishnas, including areas adjacent to the fairgrounds that received pedestrian traffic. Justice White concluded that the Krishnas were not entitled to an exception to the regulation simply because theirs was religious conduct. [69]

The Court encountered a variation on the same theme six years later in *Board of Airport Commissioners v. Jews for Jesus (1987)*. [70] The issue presented in this case concerned the constitutionality of a resolution passed by the Los Angeles Board of Airport Commissioners in July 1983 that prohibited the use of the central airport terminal area for all "First Amendment activities." [71] Alan Howard Snyder, a minister of the Gospel for Jews for Jesus, was asked by airport security officials to leave the Los Angeles airport in July 1984 for distributing religious materials in the central terminal area. The security guard told Snyder that he would be arrested and subject to legal action if he did not cease distributing the literature. Although Snyder had previously proselytized at the Los Angeles airport, he did not protest the request for him to leave the airport terminal.

Snyder and Jews for Jesus, Inc., immediately contested the resolution in federal district court as facially violative of both the California and United States Constitutions. Jews for Jesus argued that the airport's total ban on "First Amendment" activities denied them lawful access to a public forum. The plaintiffs also argued that the regulation had been applied to them in a discriminatory manner, cutting at the heart of their religious mission of proselytizing. The trial court held that the central terminal area of the Los Angeles airport qualified as a traditional public forum open to citizen access for religious and political purposes and that the airport resolution was facially unconstitutional under the free speech clause of the First Amendment of the United States Constitution. It did not reach the other questions presented. The Ninth Circuit Court of Appeals affirmed. [72]

Writing for a unanimous Court, Justice O'Connor agreed with the lower courts that the airport constituted a traditional public forum and that the ban amounted to a facial violation of the First Amendment. Justice O'Connor held that the overbreadth doctrine of the First Amendment barred such an ordinance because it "reaches the universe of expressive activity. [B]y prohibiting all protected expression, [the ordinance] purports to create a virtual 'First Amendment Free Zone' at LAX. . .of not just the activity of respondents; it prohibits talking and reading, or the wearing of campaign buttons or symbolic clothing." [73] Justice O'Connor concluded that, even if the Los Angeles airport were not a public forum, "no conceivable interest would justify such an absolute prohibition of speech." [74]

Religious Discrimination in the Marketplace

The law prohibiting religious discrimination in the economic marketplace is primarily anchored in two sources: the religion clauses of the First Amendment and the Civil Rights Act of 1964. [75]

Government Action

From *Cantwell* through the early 1960s, litigation brought under the free exercise clause primarily involved challenges to government regulations that burdened religious practices and conduct in public places [76] or conflicted with the civil obligations of citizens to government. [77] Constitutional litigation challenging state action that resulted in adverse economic consequences for members of minority religions in the marketplace did not receive adjudication in the Supreme Court until 1961, when the Court decided the *Sunday Closing Cases*. [78] The issues in these four separate cases focused on the Sunday "blue" laws in four states which required merchants to either close, or limited the products that could be sold, on Sundays. For those merchants whose religious beliefs mandated they refrain from commercial activity on Saturday, the regulations posed a significant economic hardship. In all four cases, the Court ruled that while such statutes did indeed make the religious observances of Saturday Sabbatarians "more expensive," none violated the religion clauses. Two of those cases, *Braunfeld v. Brown* and *Gallagher v. Crown Kosher Super Market*, were instituted by Orthodox Jewish merchants who argued that forcing them to close on Sunday amounted to state-sanctioned punishment for remaining true to their religious beliefs.

Chief Justice Earl Warren wrote that the legislature possessed the legitimate power to enact closing laws that promoted the secular purpose of "providing a day of rest" to "eliminate the atmosphere of commercial noise and activity." [79] Concluding his opinion, the Chief Justice held such statutes were "valid despite [their] indirect burden on religious observance unless the State may accomplish its purpose by means which do not impose such a burden." [80] In this case, Chief Justice Warren ruled that no alternative means were available to the state with which to achieve it legislative purpose. [81]

Justice Brennan and Justice Potter Stewart, filing separate dissents, argued that the closing laws forced upon the merchants the cruel choice of adhering to their religious faith or securing their economic survival. Sensitive to the religious obligations of Orthodox Jews, Justice Brennan wrote that such laws entailed drastic consequences for the merchants who observed their Sabbath on Saturday, and would face the decision of whether to sacrifice the central tenets of their faith in order to avoid economic injury. [82] In language significant for the influence that it would have in future decisions, Justice Brennan suggested that the Court reconsider the standard by which it judged such statutes. Justice Brennan argued that the Court should begin to incorporate into its jurisprudence the requirement that government regulations which burdened religious conduct be held to a more exacting standard of judicial review. [83]

Justice Stewart was more direct. Agreeing with Justice Brennan that the state had "passed a law which compels an Orthodox Jew to choose between his religious faith and his economic survival," Justice Stewart, in uncharacteristic anger, wrote that it "was a cruel choice. . . [that] no state can constitutionally demand." [84] Justice Stewart accused the Court of upholding a statutory scheme that "grossly violates [the merchants'] free exercise of religion." [85]

Two terms later, in *Sherbert v. Verner (1963)*, [86] the Court effectively eviscerated the logic it relied upon in the *Sunday Closing Cases*. In the process, the Court established the constitutional foundation for the development of subsequent law protecting the rights of religious observers in the marketplace. *Sherbert* involved a challenge to a South Carolina Unemployment Compensation Commission ruling, sustained in the state supreme court, denying unemployment benefits to a Seventh-day Adventist who refused to accept employment opportunities because they would have required her to work on her Saturday Sabbath. The Supreme Court, in a landmark decision for free exercise rights, reversed the South Carolina court, holding that a state may not deny the benefits of public welfare legislation to persons who are otherwise eligible to receive them simply because of their religious convictions. Incorporating the logic and language of his *Sunday Closing Cases* dissent, Justice Brennan, writing for the 7-2 majority, held that the Commission ruling forced the plaintiff "to choose between following the precepts of her religion and forfeiting benefits, on the one hand, and abandoning one of the precepts of her religion in order to accept work, on the other hand."[87]

Articulating what is now known as the *Sherbert* test, Justice Brennan wrote that state action which burdens the religious conduct of an individual can withstand constitutional scrutiny only if the government can show that such action (1) advances a compelling state interest and (2) does so through the least restrictive means.[88] From 1963 until 1990, when *Smith* effectively overruled *Sherbert*, the compelling interest/least restrictive means test was the standard upon which the Court built and expanded its constitutional jurisprudence in cases involving governmental action having implications for religious free exercise.[89] For nearly twenty years, the *Sherbert* test shielded religious minorities from most state action having deleterious consequences for their livelihood in the secular world. That is the reason why the sudden turnaround of the Court in *Oregon v. Smith* has caused such widespread alarm.

The initial reaffirmation of *Sherbert* in the employment and hiring arena came at the outset of the decade in *Thomas v. Review Board (1981).*[90] In *Thomas*, a Jehovah's Witness quit his job when his employer transferred him to another position in the company that was responsible for manufacturing armaments. Thomas, arguing that his religious and philosophical opposition to war precluded him from accepting the assignment, quit his job. His application for unemployment benefits was denied by the Review Board of the Indiana Employment Security Division, which ruled that Thomas had left his job on the basis of philosophical differences, not reasons that were "objectively job-related."[91]

The Supreme Court, in an 8-1 opinion authored by Chief Justice Burger, overruled the Indiana Review Board, holding that the denial of unemployment benefits to Thomas violated the *Sherbert* standard. The Chief Justice reiterated that, under *Sherbert*, state action infringing on free exercise rights must advance a substantial governmental interest to justify the resulting burden on religious conduct. The Chief Justice wrote that "a person may not be compelled to choose between the exercise of a First Amendment right and participation in an otherwise available public program [when] the infringement upon free exercise is substantial."[92]

The sole dissenter, Justice Rehnquist, argued that *Sherbert* should be overruled. Justice Rehnquist accused the Court of overextending its interpretation of the free exercise clause far beyond what it was designed to protect and argued that it should have used *Thomas* to reevaluate its jurisprudence in this area. He maintained that the free exercise clause afforded constitutional protection to individual religious beliefs, not to religious conduct. The free exercise clause could not, under any condition, be construed to entitle individuals to state benefits.[93]

Justice Rehnquist dissented again on similar grounds when the Court once more reaffirmed *Sherbert* six years later in *Hobbie v. Unemployment Appeals Commission (1987).*[94] There, the Court confronted a question almost identical to the one it decided in *Sherbert*, but with one factual variation.

Paula Hobbie was employed as an assistant manager for a Florida jewelry store chain. Hobbie had worked for Lawton & Company, which owned the chain, for over two years when she underwent a religious conversion and became a Seventh-day Adventist. As a newly observant Saturday Sabbatarian, Hobbie could no longer work on Friday nights or Saturdays, as she had done prior to her conversion. Hobbie then worked out a new arrangement with her immediate supervisor, who reassigned her to work on Sundays. This agreement presented no problems for several weeks until it came to the attention of the parent company. Lawton employment policies required that Hobbie work on Saturdays, and she was soon ordered to discontinue her new schedule. When she refused, Paula Hobbie was fired.

The Florida Department of Labor denied Hobbie's application for unemployment compensation, ruling that individuals who have been fired due to work-related "misconduct" were not eligible under Florida law. Her appeals through state administrative and judicial proceedings all failed. [95] Each time, the state argued that *Sherbert* and *Thomas* were inapplicable to Hobbie's case because she, and not her employer, had created the conditions for dismissal when her religious conversion took place after she began working. Thus, the Court would have to decide, as Florida contended, whether *Sherbert* protected individuals whose religious needs arose after a substantial period of employment from receiving state benefits.

By an 8-1 margin, the Supreme Court reversed the decision below, ruling that the timing of an individual's religious affiliation is constitutionally irrelevant. Justice Brennan, relying squarely on *Sherbert* and *Thomas*, rejected the arguments of the Florida Unemployment Appeals Commission, holding that "no meaningful distinction" existed in *Hobbie* that set it apart from the previous two cases. [96] Referring to the argument proffered by the Commission that Hobbie disqualified herself under *Sherbert* because she acted as the "agent of change," Justice Brennan wrote that the "timing of Hobbie's conversion is immaterial to our determination that her free exercise rights have been burdened. The First Amendment protects the free exercise rights of employees who adopt religious beliefs or convert to another after they are hired." [97]

The Court rejected another attempt to chip away at the *Sherbert* test two years later when it addressed the question of whether an individual whose religious beliefs forbid him from working on Sunday, but who is not affiliated with a recognized religious denomination, was eligible for unemployment compensation. The issue in *Frazee v. Illinois Department of Employment Security (1989)* [98] centered on the refusal of William Frazee, a self-proclaimed Christian who professed no affiliation to an organized religious denomination, to accept a position secured for him by a temporary employment agency which required him to work on Saturdays. Under Illinois Department of Employment Security regulations, Frazee's refusal to work was without the requisite "good cause" necessary to qualify him for unemployment compensation. Consequently, he was denied relief. On appeal, the Illinois Court of Appeals affirmed, holding that Frazee's claim did not satisfy the necessary conditions under *Sherbert* because his religious beliefs were not linked to a "tenet, belief, or teaching of an established religious sect." [99] Upon refusal of the Illinois Supreme Court to hear the case, Frazee appealed to the United States Supreme Court.

There, a unanimous Court reversed, ruling that the denial of unemployment compensation benefits to Frazee simply because he lacked denominational affiliation violated the free exercise clause. In his opinion for the Court, Justice White found that Frazee possessed a sincere belief that his religious faith mandated that he refrain from working on Sunday and held that this claim alone was sufficient to merit the protection of the free exercise clause. [100] The fact that Frazee did not profess allegiance to a recognized religious denomination or sect was irrelevant to the burden that the Illinois Employment Security Division had placed on his free exercise rights. Justice White wrote that "while membership in a sect or religious affiliation would simplify the problem, the notion that one must respond to the commands of a particular religious organization to merit the protection of the free exercise clause must be rejected." [101]

The *Frazee* decision appeared to leave little doubt that the Court viewed the *Sherbert* rationale, which protected Sabbatarians and other minority religious observers from undue economic hardship in the economic marketplace, as firmly anchored in the moorings of the free exercise clause. The Court had indeed shown greater reluctance to extend the broad reading of the free exercise clause given in *Thomas, Hobbie and Frazee* to other, nonemployment-related conflicts between the spiritual and the secular obligations of individuals. But nothing in those or any of its other decisions provided the slightest clue that, just one year after its unanimous decision in *Frazee*, the Court would, without rhyme or reason, place its settled free exercise jurisprudence on the constitutional cutting board for wholesale reexamination.

In *Employment Division of Oregon v. Smith (1990)*, [102] the Supreme Court held that two Native Americans, dismissed from their jobs as drug counselors because of their sacramental ingestion of peyote during a church ceremony, were not entitled to unemployment compensation under the free exercise clause. The Court stressed that the law banning use of the drug applied to the entire population and did not single out the Native American church. This result could easily have been reached using the *Sherbert* test. State statutes disqualifying individuals for public welfare benefits because they refused to work on the Sabbath or refused to work with armament components could reasonably be distinguished from the requirement that drug counselors remain drug-free—even when the drug use is restricted to religious ceremonies. The Court could have also found that Oregon's interest in prohibiting drug abuse was compelling and that banning all drug use was the least restrictive means of accomplishing this state interest. Instead, the Court completely rejected the compelling interest standard.

Justice Scalia, in his opinion for the 6-3 majority, took an additional—and entirely unexpected—step and announced that the Court need not analyze the free exercise implications triggered in this case under the compelling interest/least restrictive means rationale of *Sherbert*. In a stunning departure from the settled free exercise jurisprudence of the Court covering a span of close to three decades, Justice Scalia wrote that "the *Sherbert* test [is] inapplicable" to governmental action prohibiting "across-the-board" illegal conduct, even if such action has the corollary effect of implicating the free exercise clause and, in the process, placing a significant burden on religious practices. [103] Casting doubt upon the post-*Smith* vitality of the compelling interest test in free exercise litigation, Justice Scalia contended that

> The 'compelling government interest' requirement seems benign, because it is familiar from other fields. But using it as the standard that must be met before the government may accord different treatment on the basis of race . . .or before the government may regulate the content of speech . . .is not remotely comparable to using it for the purpose asserted here. What it *produces in those other fields—equality of treatment, and an unrestricted flow of contending speech—are constitutional norms; what it would produce here—a private right to ignore generally applicable laws—is a constitutional anomaly.* [104]

> We cannot afford the luxury of deeming *presumptively invalid*, as applied to the religious objector, every regulation of conduct that does not protect an interest of the highest order. [105]

Not content with just discarding a benchmark juridical principle of the free exercise clause, Justice Scalia called into consideration the role of the courts in safeguarding the rights of religious minorities:

> To say that a nondiscriminatory religious-practice exemption is permitted, or even that it is desirable, is not to say that it is constitutionally required, and that the appropriate occasions for its creation can be discerned by the courts. It may fairly be said that leaving accommodation to the political process will place at a relative disadvantage those religious practices that are not widely engaged in; but that unavoidable consequence of democratic government must be preferred to a system in which each conscience is a law unto itself or in which judges weigh the social importance of all laws against the centrality of all religious beliefs. [106]

Concurring only in the judgment of the Court, Justice O'Connor criticized the *Smith* majority for misreading "settled First Amendment precedent" to reach its decision, which she argued could have been reached by applying "our established free exercise jurisprudence." [107] However, for all the concern Justice O'Connor professes to have for the fair and equal protection for religious minorities, her opinions lead one to believe that she is instead a velvet hammer, reaching the identical conclusions of her conservative colleagues through the guise of more enlightened means.

Justice Scalia's opinion drew a sharp dissent from Justice Blackmun. Joined by Justices Brennan and Marshall, Justice Blackmun charged the Court with "effectuat[ing] a wholesale overturning of settled law concerning the Religion Clauses of our Constitution," law that was "thought [to be] a settled and inviolate principle of this Court's free exercise jurisprudence," and law which the Court now "perfunctorily dismisses as . . .constitutional anomaly." [108] Justice Blackmun was especially troubled by the notion advanced in Justice Scalia's majority opinion that the "strict scrutiny of a state law burdening the free exercise of religion is a 'luxury' that a well-ordered society cannot afford, and that the repression of minority religions is an 'unavoidable consequence of democratic government.' " [109] Contrary to the interpretation that Justice Scalia had given the free exercise clause, Justice Blackmun wrote that "the Founders [hardly] thought their dearly bought freedom from religious persecution a 'luxury,' but an essential element of liberty—and they could not have considered religious intolerance 'unavoidable,' for they drafted the Religion Clauses precisely in order to avoid that intolerance." [110]

Congress has already moved to ameliorate the potential consequences of *Smith* for the protection of religious free exercise. In 1990, Representative Stephen J. Solarz (D-N.Y.) introduced the Religious Freedom Restoration Act, which would require courts having jurisdiction in cases involving First Amendment free exercise claims to analyze them under the compelling interest/least restrictive means test established in *Sherbert*. The legislation was conceived with the widespread support of a diverse coalition of religious organizations and secular civil liberties groups. It also has drawn numerous co-sponsors in the House of Representatives since it was first introduced. While Congress took no action in 1990, the legislation will be reintroduced in 1991.

Private Action

The passage of the Civil Rights Act of 1964 marked the first concerted attempt by Congress to bar private employers from discriminating on the basis of race, color, religion, sex or national origin in employment decisions. The provision of the Act invoked in litigation involving religiously discriminatory employment practices, Title VII, applies to private employers of more than 15 persons, labor unions and governmental entities. Litigation challenging workplace discrimination on the basis of race and gender is most responsible for the contemporary meaning of these provisions of the Civil Rights Act of 1964. But the Court has also confronted on several occasions the opportunity to define the scope of protection and legal remedies available to victims of religious discrimination in the employment arena.

In its original form, the Civil Rights Act of 1964 did not contain language requiring employers to accommodate the needs of employees unable to work on certain days because of their religious beliefs. The anti-discrimination provisions of the Act were originally intended only to prohibit private employers from using religion as a criterion in their employment and hiring decisions. However, the *Sherbert* decision soon led the federal government to put into place legal regulations designed to shield individuals against arbitrary dismissal from their jobs due to religious conflicts.

In 1968 the Equal Employment Opportunity Commission adopted a regulation which required employers to make "reasonable accommodations" to the religious needs of employees. [111] Four years later, Congress passed the Equal Employment Opportunity Act, which amended Title VII to include a requirement that private employers make "reasonable accommodation" to the needs of employees requesting alternative work arrangements on grounds which were related to their religious beliefs. [112] The 1972 congressional provision modified the "reasonable accommodation" language of the EEOC regulation to require through statute that employers make a demonstrable attempt to accommodate employee religious practices, unless the accommodation would pose an "undue burden" on business operations. [113]

The Court issued its first constitutional interpretation of the reasonable accommodation section of Title VII in *Trans World Airlines v. Hardison (1976)*. [114] Dismissing the assertion of TWA that the reasonable accommodations provision violated the establishment clause because it granted preferential treatment to employees on the basis of religion, the Court upheld the statutory scheme developed by Congress as a constitutional means through which to guard against religious discrimination in the workplace. Justice White, writing for a 7-2 majority, developed the constitutional standard for subsequent Title VII litigation on the reasonable accommodations issue, holding that employers bound by Title VII must accommodate the religious needs of their employees unless the accommodation imposed more than a *de minimis* economic burden on the employer. More than a *de minimis* burden on the employer would amount to an undue hardship. The Court held that the language in Title VII did not mandate such an obligation. [115]

Other than the vague *de minimis* standard, the Court has still not provided a clear definition of what constitutes "undue hardship" under the reasonable accommodations provision of Title VII. *Hardison* and subsequent Title VII decisions indicate that it is still formulating a constitutional standard that satisfies the competing interests involved. [116] Moreover, the Court has declined to reconsider *Hardison* in the Title VII cases that have since come before it. [117] Nonetheless, the *Hardison* standard, unlike *Sherbert*, remains good law.

The court issued several rulings during the 1980s affecting the legal obligations of employers and the rights of religious observers under Title VII of the Civil Rights Act of 1964. The results, however, are less than consistent.

In *Thorton v. Caldor (1985)*[118] and *Ansonia v. Philbrook (1986)*,[119] the Court, on the one hand, brushed aside contentious requests by employers to declare the reasonable accomodation provision of Title VII unconstitutional and, on the other hand, rejected arguments by religious employees to broaden the scope of the *Hardison* standard. The Court muddled through both cases to reach a middle ground that created new ripples, not waves, in the current application of Title VII to religious conduct in the workplace and failed to peel off the opaqueness that continues to cloud our understanding of this area of the law.

Thornton concerned an establishment clause challenge to a 1976 Connecticut statute which was part of a more comprehensive legislative effort to modify the Sunday closing laws of that state. The operative provision of the statute stated that no one could be required to work on a day he or she observes as Sabbath. After its enactment, Donald Thornton, a retail employee of Caldor, Inc., a department store chain doing business in Connecticut, asked that he no longer be assigned to work on Sunday, the day of his designated Sabbath. Caldor refused to honor his request. In the alternative, Thornton was given an assignment to work at another Caldor store, one which closed on Sunday, but that was located much farther from his old job. He was also offered a demotion to a lower-salaried, non-supervisory position within the company. Thornton rejected both options. Upon learning that he would be demoted anyway, Thornton resigned from Caldor and filed a religious discrimination suit asking for reinstatement and damages. In response, Caldor challenged the constitutionality of the Connecticut Sabbath law. It argued first that the provision mandating absolute compliance with religious observances of employees violated the establishment clause. Caldor also charged that the statute conflicted with the "undue hardship" standard of Title VII.

Writing for an 8-1 majority, Chief Justice Burger agreed with Caldor that the Connecticut statute violated the establishment clause, ruling that it conferred an "absolute" benefit to Sabbath observers at the exclusion of all other secular interests in the workplace, but refused the opportunity to comment on Title VII requirements.[120]

Justice O'Connor agreed with the Chief Justice that the Sabbath law had "an impermissible effect" of advancing religion.[121] In her concurrence, Justice O'Connor, joined by Justice Marshall, took careful steps to point out that nothing in the majority opinion suggested "that the religious accommodation provisions of Title VII of the Civil Rights Act are similarly invalid. Since Title VII calls for reasonable rather than absolute accommodation and extends that requirement to all religious beliefs and practices rather than protecting only the Sabbath observance, I believe an objective observer would perceive it as an anti-discrimination law rather than an endorsement of religion or a particular religious practice."[122]

Several religious organizations had submitted *amicus* briefs in support of the Connecticut Sabbath law, viewing it as a legitimate legislative objective to accommodate the rights of religious observers in the workplace. But the narrow reading that the Court gave the statute, with its focus on the "absolute" nature of the benefit conferred exclusively to Sabbatarians and the reassurances it provided on the constitutionality of the religious accommodation provisions of Title VII, made the

Caldor decision only a minimal disappointment. The same cannot be said for *Ansonia.*

Ronald Philbrook, a business and typing teacher at Ansonia High School in Ansonia, Connecticut, was a member of the Worldwide Church of God, whose religious beliefs require that he miss a number of days from work to attend worship services. Since the number of absences exceeded his allowance of paid leave days, Philbrook had his salary docked for many of these absences. When his faithful observance of religious holidays became too costly, Philbrook petitioned the school board to accommodate him through one of two alternative arrangements that he suggested would allow him to meet his employee obligations without compromising his religious commitments. Noting that the collective bargaining agreement of the teachers' union permitted three days of each school year to be used for religious holiday leave and granted three additional days leave for personal business, all of which were fully paid, Philbrook suggested that he be allowed to use the personal leave for religious holiday observance. As an alternative, Philbrook offered to pay a substitute to teach in his absence, which would cost him less than losing a full day's pay. Both offers were rejected, leading Philbrook to sue the Ansonia School Board for failure to accommodate his religious needs under Title VII.

A federal district court ruled against Philbrook, finding that he had failed to prove religious discrimination because he had not lost his job. On appeal, the Second Circuit Court of Appeals reversed and remanded for rehearing, ruling that a loss of employment is not necessary to show a violation of Title VII and also that Philbrook had indeed proven religious discrimination. [123] The Second Circuit also held that, under Title VII, employers are required to accept an employee's accommodation proposal unless it causes undue hardship, a much more expansive reading than the federal courts had previously given to the "reasonable accommodation" provision of that statute. [124]

But the Supreme Court, in a 7-2 decision, overruled the Second Circuit, holding that neither the terms nor the legislative history of Title VII supported the conclusion of the Second Circuit that employers had a statutory obligation to accept an employee's proposal for religious accommodation in the workplace. [125] While this holding disappointed those who supported Philbrook's claim, the decision upheld without a doubt the obligation of employers to make "reasonable accommodations" for their religious employees. Writing for the Court, Justice Rehnquist wrote that "where the employer has already reasonably accommodated the employee's religious needs, the statutory inquiry is at an end. The employer need not further show that each of the employee's alternative accommodations would result in undue hardship." [126]

However, the Court noted that the alternatives offered by Philbrook were "reasonable," and stated that the operative question was the reasonableness of the school's accommodation offer. The case was remanded to the district court for further factfinding on the merits of the leave provisions of the collective bargaining agreement, which disallowed the use of business leave for religious purposes. "Unpaid leave is not a reasonable accommodation when paid leave is provided for all purposes except religious ones," wrote Justice Rehnquist. [127] Continuing, Justice Rehnquist wrote "such an arrangement would display a discrimination against religious practices that is the antithesis of reasonableness." [128] Nonetheless, the Court sidestepped the chance to refine the *Hardison* rule.

That same term, a unanimous Court rejected an establishment clause challenge to a provision of Title VII permitting religious entities to discriminate on the basis of religion in non-faith related employment decisions. Section 702 of Title VII excludes religious institutions from the anti-discrimination provisions of the statute "with respect to the employment of individuals of a particular religion to perform work connected with the carrying on by such corporation, association, educational institution, or society of its activities." [129] Originally, Section 702 applied only to employees hired expressly for positions related directly to the religious functions of the employer. In 1972, Congress amended Section 702 to permit religious institutions to discriminate on religious grounds in their employment and hiring decisions, including non-faith related jobs.

In *Corporation of the Presiding Bishop of the Church of Jesus Christ of Latter-day Saints v. Amos (1987),* [130] the Court reversed the decision of the federal district court in Utah, which had found Section 702 to violate the establishment clause. Writing for the Court, Justice White held that when Christine Amos, who, along with several other individuals employed by the Mormon Church in non-faith related positions, was fired for not meeting the religious standards of the church, she had no cause of action under Title VII. In amending Section 702 to shield religious institutions from the provisions applicable to all other employers covered by the Civil Rights Act, the Court ruled that Congress had acted within its permissible legislative purpose "to alleviate significant governmental interference with the ability of religious organizations to define and carry out their religious missions." [131]

Distinguishing the challenge brought against Section 702 in *Amos* from the issues raised in *Caldor,* the Court noted that the Connecticut statute found unconstitutional in *Caldor* involved several major differences from the attack mounted on Title VII in *Amos.* In *Caldor,* the Court struck down the Sabbath law on the grounds that it placed the "force of law" behind the employer's obligation to accommodate religious observers. The Court ruled in *Amos* that Section 702 did not place an affirmative mandate through statute on religious institutions to discharge nonaffiliated persons, but instead released religious employers from regulations that could excessively entangle them with the state. [132]

Conclusion

Freedom of religion, once considered sacrosanct among the fundamental freedoms entitled to vigorous judicial protection against majoritarian rule, enters the 1990s relegated to the unaccustomed and unforseen position of second-class stature in our constellation of constitutional values. The historical evolution of the First Amendment free exercise clause in the modern judicial era had breathed real life into the parchment promise of religious freedom for minorities, and further strengthened the rights of all individuals to believe and practice their religious beliefs free from government intrusion. The *Smith* decision effectively demolishes the constitutional protection that, for the better part of four decades, had shielded unorthodox religious conduct from the legislative will of intolerant majorities. [133]

The Court did not undercut the minimal protection extended to religious minorities through the religious accommodation provisions of Title VII of the Civil Rights Act of 1964, despite the crabbed reading it has given to the language protecting religious observers in the workplace, but it provided little indication that an extension of the *Hardison* rule occupied a significant place among its immediate or future concerns. Given the new, uncertain direction of the religion clause jurisprudence of the Court, the likelihood that religious minorities stand to benefit from innovative legal doctrine broadening the rights of minority religious observers in the workplace appears to be minimal. *Smith* has no direct impact on the Title VII religious accommodation decisions of the Court, but its tenor does raise the possibility that *Hardison*, too, may be in for a constitutional winnowing.[134] How these and future free exercise cases are decided will provide greater insight into the magnitude of *Smith* for the rights of religious minorities in all facets of American life.

[1] 310 U.S. 296 (1940).

[2] Id. at 303.

[3] Id. at 303-04.

[4] Id. at 304.

[5] *E.g., Frazee v. Illinois Department of Employment Security*, 109 S. Ct. 1514 (1989); *Hobbie v. Employment Commission*, 480 U.S. 136 (1987); *Ansonia v. Philbrook*, 499 U.S. 60 (1986); *Thomas v. Review Board of Indiana*, 450 U.S. 772 (1981); *Sherbert v. Verner*, 374 U.S. 348 (1963).

[6] 319 U.S. 624 (1943).

[7] Id. at 638.

[8] 450 U.S. 707 (1981).

[9] Id. at 718, quoting *Wisconsin v. Yoder*, 406 U.S. 205, 215 (1972).

[10] Especially noteworthy is *Wisconsin v. Yoder*, 406 U.S. 205 (1972) (held that compelling Amish children to comply with compulsory state education laws requiring school attendance until the age of sixteen violated the free exercise clause).

[11] 110 S. Ct. 1595 (1990).

[12] Id. at 1603-06.

[13] Id. at 1606 (emphasis added).

[14] 475 U.S. 503 (1986).

[15] Id. at 505 (statute cited in text).

[16] 530 F. Supp. 12 (D.D.C. 1981).

[17] *Goldman v. Secretary of Defense*, 734 F.2d 1531 (D.C. Cir. 1984).

[18] *Goldman*, 475 U.S. at 508-9.

[19] Id.

[20] Id. at 510-11 (Justice Stevens, concurring).

[21] Id. at 513.

[22] Id. at 514 (Justice Brennan, dissenting).

[23] Id.

[24] Id. at 516.

[25] Id.

[26] Id. at 521.

[27] Department of Defense Directive No. 1300.17 (Feb. 3, 1988).

[28] 482 U.S. 342 (1987).

[29] *Shabazz v. O'Lone*, 595 F. Supp. 928 (D.N.J. 1984).

[30] Id. at 934.

[31] Id.

[32] *Shabazz v. O'Lone*, 782 F.2d 416 (3d Cir. 1986).

[33] Id. at 420.

[34] *O'Lone v. Shabazz*, 482 U.S. 342, 353 (1987).

[35] Id. at 356 (Justice Brennan, dissenting).

[36] Id. at 368.

[37] 108 S. Ct. 1319 (1988).

[38] Id. at 1322.

[39] Id.

[40] *Northwest Indian Cemetery Protective Association v. Peterson*, 565 F. Supp. 586 (N.D. Cal. 1983).

[41] *Northwest Indian Cemetery Protective Association v. Peterson*, 795 F.2d 688 (9th Cir. 1986).

[42] Justice Kennedy did not hear or take part in the case.

[43] *Lyng v. Northwest Indian Cemetery Protective Association*, 108 S. Ct. 1319, 1325 (1988).

[44] Id. at 1326.

[45] Id. at 1327.

[46] *Smith*, 110 S. Ct. at 1606-15 (Justice O'Connor, concurring).

[47] *Lyng*, 108 S. Ct. at 1330 (Justice Brennan, dissenting).

[48] 108 S. Ct. at 1335.

[49] Id.

[50] Id. at 1340.

[51] *Cf., Smith*, 110 S. Ct. at 1603-06, especially footnotes 2, 3, 4 and 5, in which Justice Scalia replies to the criticisms of his opinion presented in Justice O'Connor's concurrence.

[52] 683 F.2d 1030 (7th Cir. 1982).

[53] 819 F.2d 875 (9th Cir. 1987).

[54] *Menora v. Illinois High School Association*, 527 F. Supp. 637 (N.D. Ill. 1981).

[55] See Chapter Four, *supra*.

[56] *Menora*, 527 F. Supp. at 1032.

[57] Id. at 1035.

[58] Id. at 1033-34.

[59] Id. at 1035.

[60] 819 F.2d 875 (9th Cir.), *cert. denied*, 484 U.S. 926 (1987).

[61] *Paul*, 819 F.2d at 876-78 (discussing summary judgment granted by the district court).

[62] Id. at 883.

[63] Id. at 883-4.

[64] Id. at 884.

[65] *E.g., Niemotko v. Maryland*, 340 U.S. 268 (1951) (upholding right of Witnesses to proselytize in public parks); *Murdock v. Pennsylvania*, 319 U.S. 105 (1943) (striking down state law that prohibited distribution of religious materials in public places); *Cantwell v. Connecticut*, 310 U.S. 296 (1940) (declared that states could not bar the right of religious organizations to propagate their faith through door-to-door solicitation of religious materials).

[66] 452 U.S. 640 (1981).

[67] *ISKCON v. Heffron*, 299 N.W.2d 79 (Sup. Ct. Minn. 1980).

[68] *Heffron v. ISKCON*, 452 U.S. 640, 654 (1981).

[69] Id. at 652-3.

[70] 482 U.S. 569 (1987).

[71] Id. at 570-71.

[72] *Jews for Jesus v. Board of Airport Commissioners*, 785 F.2d 791 (9th Cir. 1986).

[73] *Board of Airport Commissioners v. Jews for Jesus*, 482 U.S. 569, 574 (1987).

[74] Id. at 575.

[75] The Civil Rights Act of 1964, 78 Stat. 241, as amended, 42 U.S.C. 2000e(j) *et. seq.* The Equal Employment Opportunity Commission soon interpreted this provision of the Civil Rights Act not only to bar employment discrimination on the basis of religion, but also to require employers to include all "aspects of religious observance and practice, as well as belief, unless an employer demonstrates that he is unable to reasonably accommodate to an employee's or prospective employee's religious observance or practice without undue hardship on the conduct of the employer's business" when making personnel decisions. Congress amended Title VII of the original 1964 Civil Rights Act in 1972 to include the "reasonable accommodation" language.

[76] See note 65, *supra*.

[77] *E.g., First Unitarian Church v. Los Angeles*, 357 U.S. 545 (1958) (declaring church compliance with county loyalty oath requirement for tax exemption to violate free exercise clause); *Witmer v. United States*, 348 U.S. 375 (1955) (upheld conscientious objection claim of a Jehovah's Witness on "ministerial exemption" grounds that made all Witnesses ineligible for military service).

[78] *Gallagher v. Crown Kosher Market*, 366 U.S. 617 (1961); *Braunfeld v. Brown*, 366 U.S. 599 (1961); *Two Guys v. McGinley*, 366 U.S. 582 (1961); *McGowan v. Maryland*, 366 U.S. 420 (1961).

[79] *Braunfeld*, 366 U.S. at 607-8.

[80] Id. at 607.

[81] Id. at 608-09.

[82] Id. at 613 (Justice Brennan, dissenting).

[83] Id. at 614-15.

[84] Id. at 616 (Justice Stewart, dissenting).

[85] Id.

[86] 374 U.S. 398 (1962).

[87] Id. at 404.

[88] Id. at 406-407.

[89] See note 5, *supra*.

[90] 450 U.S. 707 (1981).

[91] Id. at 712.

[92] Id. at 716.

[93] Id. at 722-23 (Justice Rehnquist, dissenting).

[94] 480 U.S. 136 (1987).

[95] 475 So. 2d 711 (Dist. Ct. App. Fla. 1985).

[96] *Hobbie*, 480 U.S. at 143-4.

[97] Id. at 144.

[98] 109 S. Ct. 1514 (1989).

[99] *Frazee v. Illinois Department of Employment Security*, 512 N.E.2d 789, 791 (App. Ct. Ill. 1987).

[100] *Frazee*, 109 S. Ct. at 1517-18.

[101] Id. at 1517.

[102] 110 S. Ct. 1595 (1990).

[103] Id. at 1603.

[104] Id. at 1604.

[105] Id. at 1605.

[106] Id. at 1606.

[107] Id. at 1613.

[108] Id. at 1616 (Justice Blackmun, dissenting).

[109] Id.

[110] Id.

[111] 29 C.F.R. 1605.1(b) (1968).

[112] The Equal Employment Opportunity Act of 1972, 86 Stat. 103, 42 U.S.C. 2000e, *et. seq.*

[113] The Equal Employment Opportunity Act of 1972, 86 Stat. 104- 05, 42 U.S.C. 2000e(j).

[114] 432 U.S. 63 (1977).

[115] *Hardison*, 432 U.S. at 84-85.

[116] *Ansonia v. Philbrook*, 479 U.S. 60 (1987); *see also American Postal Workers Union v. Postmaster General*, 781 F.2d 772 (9th Cir. 1986) (ruling that dismissal of two Post Office employees for refusing to hand out selective service registration forms on religious grounds, despite requests of employees for alternative work arrangements, did not violate the *Hardison* rule).

[117] *Thornton v. Caldor*, 472 U.S. 703 (1985).

[118] 472 U.S. 703 (1985).

[119] 479 U.S. 60 (1986).

[120] *Thornton*, 472 U.S. at 710-11.

[121] Id. at 711 (Justice O'Connor, concurring).

[122] Id. at 711-12.

[123] *Philbrook v. Ansonia*, 757 F.2d 476, 480 (2d Cir. 1985).

[124] Id. at 484.

[125] *Ansonia v. Philbrook*, 479 U.S. 60, 68.

[126] Id.

[127] Id. at 71.

[128] Id.

[129] The Civil Rights Act of 1964, 78 Stat. 255, 42 U.S.C. 2000e-1.

[130] 594 F. Supp. 791 (D. Utah 1984), *reversed*, 483 U.S. 327 (1987).

[131] *Amos*, 483 U.S. at 339.

[132] Id.

[133] The impact of *Smith* in subsequent free exercise litigation has already been felt, as several actions taken by the Supreme Court since make clear. *See, e.g., First Covenant Church v. City of Seattle*, 787 P.2d 1352 (Sup. Ct. Wash. 1990), *cert. granted, judgment vacated and remanded*, 111 S. Ct. 1097 (1991) (vacated a Washington Supreme Court decision that held the application of Seattle's Landmark Preservation Ordinance to churches violative of the free exercise clause and ordered the case to be reconsidered under the *Smith* rule); *St. Bartholomew's Church v. City of New York*, 914 F.2d 348 (1990), *cert. denied*, 111 S. Ct. 1103 (1991) (rejecting free exercise claim and permitting government to require church-owned buildings to comply with municipal landmarking ordinances); *Minnesota v. Hershberger*, 444 N.W.2d 282 (Sup. Ct. Minn. 1989), *cert. granted and judgment vacated*, 110 S. Ct. 1918 (1990), *remand*, 426 N.W.2d 393 (Sup. Ct. Minn. 1990) (ordering Minnesota Supreme Court to reconsider whether free exercise clause permits Amish to exempt their horse- drawn buggies from state statute requiring display of flourescent orange triangle on slow-moving vehicles; the Minnesota Supreme Court reheard the case and ruled on behalf of the Amish, but on state constitutional grounds).

[134] Federal legislation is now being considered which would address the *Hardison* standard and reverse the *Philbrook* decision.

CHAPTER SIX

CONCLUSION:
THE COURT AND
THE RELIGION CLAUSES

The period from 1980-1990 will be remembered as one in which established constitutional doctrine interpreting the meaning of the First Amendment religion clauses underwent profound and important alteration. A reconstituted Supreme Court had come to mirror in large measure the dramatic changes that took place in the American political environment during the decade. Under its auspices, the libertarian principles for which the First Amendment religion clauses stand, those which bar the government from preferring one religion over another, assisting or inhibiting the mission of organized religion or intervening in the free exercise of individual religious beliefs, took a decided turn for the worse. As undesirable as many of the church-state decisions of the Supreme Court were during this period for their impact on public policy, equally if not more disconcerting were the energetic, provocative and occasionally nonsensical arguments coming from academic circles and elsewhere contending that these decisions and the jurisprudence used to reach them represented an important and long overdue return to the original meaning of the religion clauses.

The arguments advanced in support of a nonpreferential reading of the First Amendment religion clauses represented just a fraction of the much larger debate that came to the fore during the 1980s over the meaning of the Constitution. Since the great Chief Justice John Marshall first gave explicit recognition to the authority of courts to review the constitutional fitness of executive and legislative action in *Marbury v. Madison*,[1] judicial power has been used and misused to further the political ends of those in whose hands it rests, as well as to discern the meaning of the Constitution. Given the enormous stakes involved in the exercise of judicial power, it comes as no surprise that a continual and often vigorous debate has existed without interruption since *Marbury* over how to interpret the Constitution. Also inescapable is the fact that the intellectual polemics over constitutional interpretation often become overshadowed by the constitutional politics that flow from them, as happened during the period from 1980-1990.

It is difficult to pinpoint the moment at which the unusually passionate debate over constitutional interpretation became such a central component of public discourse during the decade. Arguments over the proper role of history in constitutional interpretation, the obligation of judges to confine themselves to the constitutional text in interpreting the document, and the relevance of original intent in deciphering the meaning of the Constitution had long occupied a significant place in academic dialogue. It is nothing short of remarkable that those arguments found a path into our public discourse, convulsed our politics with such verve, and forced participants on all sides of the debate to reexamine their fundamental understanding of the American constitutional and political tradition.

One protagonist responsible for bringing forward the public exchange over constitutional interpretation was not a writer or commentator from the influential academic and legal circles in which this debate had simmered for years, but was then U.S. Attorney General Edwin Meese III. In a 1985 address to the American Bar Association, Attorney General Meese called for judges to return to "a jurisprudence of original intention," in their interpretation of the Constitution and argued that the exercise of judicial power in the modern constitutional era had failed to respect the original design of the Framers. [2] Strange as it was for the Attorney General of the United States to call into question in full public view the worth of our constitutional jurisprudence, even more unusual was the response that his remarks generated from a sitting Supreme Court Justice, William J. Brennan. In a speech given at Georgetown University shortly after Attorney General Meese's address to the American Bar Association, Justice Brennan rejected his call for a return to "a jurisprudence of original intention" in candid and even hostile terms, arguing that "it is arrogant to pretend that from our vantage we can gauge accurately the intent of the framers. . . . Those who would restrict claims of right to the values of 1789 specifically articulated in the Constitution, turn a blind eye to social progress and eschew adaptation of overarching principles to changes of social circumstances." [3]

The Meese-Brennan exchange painted over the broad canvas of American constitutional law, but front and center in this debate were vastly different visions over the meaning of the First Amendment religion clauses and the constitutional place of religion in American public life. Throughout his thirty-four year career on the Supreme Court, Justice Brennan remained in the vanguard against frequent and sometimes clever attempts to encroach upon the constitutional principles of church-state separation and religious freedom enshrined in the First Amendment, authoring several important opinions decided under each of the religion clauses [4] and issuing poignant dissents in numerous others. [5] On the other hand, Attorney General Meese assumed the political mantle for the nonpreferentialists in the debate over the establishment clause, giving several public speeches in which he called on the Court to reconsider its church-state jurisprudence in light of the Framers' original understanding. He argued this meant prohibiting "the establishment of a particular religion or a particular church, favoring one church, or one church group over another [and did not] preclude federal aid to religious groups so long as that assistance furthered a public purpose and so long as it did not discriminate in favor of one religious group against another." [6]

Furthermore, Meese argued that the high wall of separation which the Supreme Court had built to respect the separate domains of religion and the state in the years after *Everson v. Board of Education* [7] had not, in fact, furthered the cause of religious freedom, but had instead fostered a climate of government hostility towards religion. The nonpreferentialists, including those writing from on and off the judicial bench, maintain that government accommodation of private religious beliefs in the public sphere and neutral funding schemes that aid religion without regard to denominational preference are consistent with this vision of the establishment clause, which, they argue, reflects the original design of the Framers. [8]

Too often, however, the nonpreferentialists have used the cloak of constitutional prerogative to disguise the advancement of a sectarian policy agenda, one that urges government support for religious doctrine in the public schools and government financial aid to parochial institutions, as if judicial humility, and not political enthusiasm, mandates this interpretive approach. These claims have been thoroughly rebutted by constitutional historians, [9] prominent church-state attorneys [10] and legal academics [11] whose views differ on the limits which the First Amendment imposes on the relationship between religion and the state, but agree that the Framers never intended to permit nonpreferential support for and aid to religion. Indeed, one prominent legal commentator has written that the "nonpreferentialist account flies in the face of the data. Nonpreferentialism was the last compromise offered by the defenders of establishment, and the founding generation repeatedly rejected it." [12]

In addition to their false historical claims of original intent, the nonpreferentialists have argued that the separationist decisions of the Warren Court and the early Burger Court resulted in a moral climate hostile to religion, one in which the secularization of public life became paramount to a respect for the American religious heritage and its historical place in our civic culture. As discussed in earlier chapters, the political configuration behind the drive to reintroduce religion in the public schools, to urge municipalities to support seasonal religious displays and to obtain government aid for parochial institutions consisted, for the most part, of evangelical and fundamentalist religious groups which advocated a return to this historical vision of the Framers. The more forceful among them have argued that allegiance to the metaphorical wall of separation, which the strict separationists maintain is the essence of the First Amendment, promotes a civic environment in which the forces of "irreligion" are preferred over those of religion. [13] To nonpreferenialists, the current movement towards lenient government accommodation of religion in public life represents a much overdue correction of constitutional interpretation and a period of healing for our civic culture.

These charges are not only plainly and utterly false, but are also insensitive to those who have fought long and hard for the effectuation of the constitutional promises embodied in the First Amendment religion clauses. Strict separationism does not have its moral anchor in "irreligion," but rather seeks to ensure that all individuals, regardless of their denominational or religious affiliation, remain free from the unequal burden and sense of isolation that government preferences for certain segments of organized religion impose upon those who are not among the beneficiaries. Moreover, nothing in the religion clauses prohibits individuals from incorporating their religious values into the conduct of their personal and civic life. Indeed, Alexis de Tocqueville noted the moral value of religion in tempering the individual and collective excess of democratic societies, writing that "[o]ne cannot therefore say that in the United States religion influences the laws or political opinions in detail, but it does direct mores and . . . helps to regulate the state." [14]

This Tocquevillian understanding of the American cultural and constitutional relationship between religion and civil government offers much to students of the current debate over church-state relations. It requires an almost chimerical understanding of the rich, multi-religious, multi-denominational tradition of organized American religion to believe that the Constitution requires—in fact, even makes possible—the accommodation of an ecumenical religious tradition in our public life. It does not. The Framers themselves recognized that the growing denominational pluralism among American Protestantism alone, not to mention the small but growing number of Catholics, Jews and other religions in the founding era made constitutionalized religious establishments impossible, [15] as it did restrictions on individual conscience and the free exercise of religious beliefs, including conduct linked to those beliefs. [16] When one considers that the diverse, plural character of American religious life has since expanded to include faiths, sects and religions such as Christian Scientists, Jehovah's Witnesses, Mormons and non-Western religions which were not present when the First Amendment was ratified, it becomes even more nonsensical to argue that government has an affirmative obligation to nurture and support pan-Protestant religious values, at the expense of all others, in our public life.

Nonetheless, this is the road on which the Supreme Court chose to travel during the 1980s. Placing in moral escrow the elemental American constitutional principle that to secure certain rights it is necessary to remove their fate from the whim of majoritarian bodies, the Court transgressed the design and meaning of the First Amendment to permit greater government accommodation for the interests of majoritarian religion while reducing to perilous levels the protection accorded to religious free exercise. Religious minorities have come out on the short end on both counts, having witnessed their rightful place as equals under the American Constitution recede into the mists. Such is the current state of the religion clauses, their robust interpretation no longer commanding under a Supreme Court, to paraphrase James Madison, ever less vigilant in its zeal to "take alarm at the first experiment with our liberties." [17]

[1] 5 U.S. (1 Cranch) 137 (1803).

[2] Edwin Meese III, "Speech to the American Bar Association," Washington, D.C., July 9, 1985.

[3] William J. Brennan, "Speech to Georgetown University Law School," Washington, D.C., October 12, 1985.

[4] *E.g., Edwards v. Aguillard*, 482 U.S. 578 (1987); *Aguilar v. Felton*, 473 U.S. 402 (1985); *Sherbert v. Verner*, 374 U.S. 348 (1963).

[5] *E.g., Allegheny v. ACLU*, 109 S. Ct. 3086 (1989); *Lyng v. Northwest Indian Cemetery Protective Association*, 108 S. Ct. 1319 (1988); *Goldman v. Weinberger*, 475 U.S. 503 (1986); *Lynch v. Donnelly*, 465 U.S. 668 (1984).

[6] Edwin Meese III, "Address to the Christian Legal Society," San Diego, CA, September 29, 1985.

[7] 330 U.S. 1 (1947).

[8] *See, e.g.*, Robert L. Cord, *Separation of Church and State: Historical Fact and Current Fiction* (1982); Walter Berns, *The First Amendment and the Future of American Democracy* (1978); Michael J. Malbin, *Religion and Politics: The Intentions of the Authors of the First Amendment* (1978); and Chester J. Antieau, *Freedom From Federal Establishment: Formation and Early History of the First Amendment Religious Clauses* (1964).

[9] *See* Leonard W. Levy, *The Establishment Clause: Religion and the First Amendment* (1986).

[10] *See* Leo Pfeffer, *Church, State and Freedom* (1967).

[11] *See* Douglas Laycock, "Original Intent and the Constitution Today," *The First Freedom: Religion and the Bill of Rights* 87-112, James E. Wood, Jr., ed., (1990); Laycock, *Non-Preferential Aid to Religion: A False Claim About Original Intent*, 27 William and Mary Law Review 875-923 (1986).

[12] Laycock, "Original Intent and the Constitution," *supra*, at 92.

[13] The prominent nonpreferentialist cleric, Richard John Neuhaus, expresses this view with particular ardor. *See The Naked Public Square* (1984).

[14] Tocqueville, *Democracy in America* at 291.

[15] For an exhaustive examination of the debate over religious establishments in the founding era, *see* Levy, *The Establishment Clause. See also* James E. Wood, Jr., "Religion and the Constitution," in *The First Freedom, supra*, at 1-15, who notes that the dissenting Protestants of this period, including Baptists, Methodists, Presbyterians, Quakers and Unitarians, were among the most vigorous advocates of "what would become the religion clauses of the First Amendment."

[16] *See* Michael McConnell, *The Origins and Historical Understandings of Free Exercise of Religion*, 103 Harvard Law Review 1410-1517 (May 1990).

[17] James Madison, *Memorial and Remonstrance Against Religious Assessments*, June 20, 1785.

TABLE OF CASES

Cantwell v. Connecticut, 310 U.S. 296 (1940)

Clark v. Dallas Independent School Dist., 880 F.2d 411 (5th Cir. 1989)

Clergy and Laity Concerned v. Chicago Board of Education, 586 F. Supp. 1408 (N.D. Ill. 1984)

Corporation of the Presiding Bishop of the Church of Jesus Christ of Latter-day Saints v. Amos, 483 U.S. 327 (1987)

County of Allegheny v. American Civil Liberties Union, 492 U.S. 573 (1989)

Earley v. DiCenso, 403 U.S. 602 (1971)

Edwards v. Aguillard, 482 U.S. 578 (1987)

Employment Division of Oregon v. Smith, 110 S. Ct. 1595 (1990)

Engel v. Vitale, 370 U.S. 421 (1962)

Epperson v. Arkansas, 393 U.S. 421 (1968)

Everson v. Board of Education, 330 U.S. 1 (1947)

First Covenant Church v. City of Seattle, 787 P.2d 1352 (Sup. Ct. Wash. 1990), *cert. granted, judgment vacated and remanded*, 111 S. Ct. 1097 (1991)

First Unitarian Church v. Los Angeles, 357 U.S. 545 (1958)

Florey v. Sioux Falls School District, 619 F.2d 1311 (8th Cir.), *cert. denied*, 449 U.S. 987 (1980)

Frazee v. Illinois Department of Employment Security, 489 U.S. 829 (1989)

Gallagher v. Crown Kosher Market, 366 U.S. 617 (1961)

Garnett v. Renton Area School District, 874 F.2d 608 (9th Cir. 1989)

Goldman v. Weinberger, 475 U.S. 503 (1986)

Grand Rapids v. Ball, 473 U.S. 373 (1985)

Heffron v. International Society for Krishna Consciousness, 452 U.S. 640 (1981)

Hobbie v. Employment Commission, 480 U.S. 136 (1987)

Jager v. Douglas County School District, 862 F.2d 824 (11th Cir. 1989), *cert. denied*, 490 U.S. 1090 (1989)

Kunz v. New York, 340 U.S. 290 (1951)

Larkin v. Grendel's Den, 459 U.S. 116 (1982)

Lemon v. Kurtzman, 403 U.S. 602 (1971)

Levitt v. PEARL, 413 U.S. 472 (1973)

Lubavitch of Iowa, Inc. v. Walters, 684 F. Supp. 610 (D. Iowa), *aff'd*, 808 F.2d 656 (8th Cir. 1988)

Lubbock Civil Liberties Union v. Lubbock Independent School District, 669 F.2d 1038 (5th Cir. 1982), *cert. denied*, 459 U.S. 1159 (1983)

Sherbert v. Verner, 374 U.S. 398 (1963)

Smith v. Board of School Commissioners, 827 F.2d 684 (11th Cir. 1987)

Sloan v. Lemon, 413 U.S. 825 (1973)

St. Bartholomew's Church v. City of New York, 914 F.2d 348 (2d Cir. 1990), *cert. denied*, 111 S. Ct. 1103 (1991)

Stone v. Graham, 449 U.S. 39 (1980)

Swaggert v. Board of Equalization, 110 S. Ct. 688 (1990)

Texas Monthly v. Bullock, 489 U.S. 1 (1989)

Thomas v. Review Board of Indiana, 450 U.S. 772 (1981)

Thornton v. Caldor, 472 U.S. 703 (1985)

Tilton v. Richardson, 403 U.S. 672 (1971)

Torcaso v. Watkins, 367 U.S. 488 (1961)

Trans World Airlines. v. Hardison, 432 U.S. 63 (1977)

Two Guys v. McGinley, 366 U.S. 582 (1961)

United States v. Lee, 455 U.S. 252 (1982)

United States v. Seeger, 380 U.S. 163 (1965)

United States v. Sisson, 399 U.S. 267 (1970)

Wallace v. Jaffree, 472 U.S. 38 (1985)

Walz v. Tax Commission, 397 U.S. 664 (1970)

Weisman v. Lee, 908 F.2d 1090 (1st Cir. 1990), *cert. granted*, 111 S. Ct. 1305 (1991) (No. 90-1014)

Welsh v. United States, 398 U.S. 333 (1970)

West Virginia State Board of Education v. Barnette, 319 U.S. 624 (1943)

Wheeler v. Barrera, 417 U.S. 402 (1974)

Widmar v. Vincent, 454 U.S. 263 (1981)

Wisconsin v. Yoder, 406 U.S. 205 (1972)

Witmer v. United States, 348 U.S. 375 (1955)

Witters v. Washington, 474 U.S. 481 (1986)

Wolman v. Walter, 433 U.S. 229 (1977)

Wooley v. Maynard, 430 U.S. 705 (1977)